CW00556581

ONCE UPON A STORY TIME

Edited by

Becki Mee

First published in Great Britain in 2000 by
POETRY NOW
Remus House,
Coltsfoot Drive,
Woodston,
Peterborough, PE2 9JX
Telephone (01733) 898101
Fax (01733) 313524

HB ISBN 0754308413
SB ISBN 0754308421

FOREWORD

Although we are a nation of poets we are accused of not reading poetry, or buying poetry books. After many years of listening to the incessant gripes of poetry publishers, I can only assume that the books they publish, in general, are books that most people do not want to read.

Poetry should not be obscure, introverted, and as cryptic as a crossword puzzle: it is the poet's duty to reach out and embrace the world.

The world owes the poet nothing and we should not be expected to dig and delve into a rambling discourse searching for some inner meaning.

The reason we write poetry (and almost all of us do) is because we want to communicate: an ideal; an idea; or a specific feeling. Poetry is as essential in communication, as a letter; a radio; a telephone, and the main criteria for selecting the poems in this anthology is very simple: they communicate.

CONTENTS

SANCTUARY

Two tracks of footprints, in soft sand,
led toward a tidal cove
where weed-wrapped rocks conceal a cave -
a sanctuary for love.

Racing the tide, footprints returned -
and other times were seen -
before the ocean washed that beach
as smooth as it had been.

A single trail, one misty morn,
led where that hazard lies,
and just the hint of human sobs
was heard with seagulls' cries.

No prints returned, before the tide,
and none again were seen
after the ocean washed that beach
as smooth as it had been.

David Hancock

MOSTAR 94

The tattered remains of a city that's died,
made real by a child and the tears in his eyes.
He holds out his hands, just for someone to hold,
for some place of safety, that's out of the cold.

Alone with his family, that were killed days before,
why would they do this? What reason? What for?
Outside is a soldier that hides in the rubble,
confused he cries out for help, he's in trouble.

The soldier stands up, for a second looks back,
for a moment exposed, in the line of attack.
A shout then went out, as the child runs toward him,
alone with the soldier, they're out in the open.

Together they fell, to live no more,
just two more dead bodies, to sweep from the floor.
Just one more bad link, in a long painful chain,
and just one more sad story, of a thousand the same!

Christopher Paul Rixon

THE DESCENT

As the sullen forest sleeps, in the moonless eventide
Not a being would advance, but deceive,
The howling of the creatures (by the mist they would hide)
And play on the mortal so naive.

Not knowing of the presence encircling its prey
The victim stands oblivious to all,
The allurement besieged as time would decay
Unacquainted of the destiny to fall.

With the presence running evident, could the victim comprehend
The fate that was to pursue?
But the creatures were motionless, they wouldn't apprehend
Emotions an intermix of two.

He ran

Through the undergrowth he hastened, yet the howling did not trail
Though the mortal blindly endured,
in the distance sound resumes, but what the noise entails
Is a summoning of fate to be lured.

The wind built up rage
The leaves were awoken, by the trees in their apparent discontent,
The mortal, the crag
And here it's never spoken . . .
The victim:

The mortal's descent.

Joseph Hardwick (16)

GIVE ME A KISS

'Give me a kiss' called the eight year old miss,
Precocious, demanding and bold;
'Give me a kiss and don't be so shy,
Tell me you love me and tell me no lie,
Kiss me and do as you're told'

He ran down the path with a gay carefree laugh
And slowly broke into a trot;
With a wave to the sky and a slap on the thigh
He galloped away up the street with a cry
'I will not, I will not, I will not'

'Give me a kiss' he sighed in her ear,
Urgently virile and strong;
'Give me a kiss and say we will wed,
Forget all the others and kiss me instead,
I promise I'll do you no wrong'

She ran from his arms and all of his charms,
Mocking and giggling loud;
She laughed in his face
And invited the chase,
But his spirit was hurt and too proud

'Give me a kiss' he moaned with a hiss,
Flesh wasted down to the bone;
'Give me a kiss and then say goodbye,
Tell me you love me before I must die,
Kiss me then leave me alone'

She wiped her eyes dry and placed with a sigh
A final kiss to his cheek,
Then softly departed
In truth broken hearted,
With nothing in life left to seek

His make believe horse had run its full course
And knew he had left her for good;
She'd love him so much
And still longed for his touch,
Would have taken him back if she could.

Edward J Butler

WITHOUT A LULLABY

A form lays between seamless cotton sheets
Diamond shaped into country lanes and meadows
Pastel painted print shows a cool, cheerful and inviting creek
The creeping stream gently whining and whirling.

Uncurling limbs stretches
Rocks and rolls
And rippling waves
Dances on the six by four Slumberland divan

Pristine lace-hemmed pillows freshly fluffed
Receives a clear head, calm and relaxed
Weighted, down and down, it sinks
Brow frownless, complexion glowing

Flicking eyelids spy a silver light, a shooting star
Falling like a waterfall
Falling into liquid warmth
Liquid darkness and another life

Sailing faster, gliding quicker
Up, up, higher, lighter
Floating, flowing, flying, the spirit zooms into flight
By the dream of the night

Down a country lane, swarming with birds, bees and butterflies
Near a crooked brook teeming with fish and children with hooks
Onwards into a comely, country cottage
Welcomed by all the comforts of home.

A log fire burning bright, hot cocoa and fleshly roasted marshmallows
                                                    by the fireside
A rocking chair, southward facing onto a landscape of soul delight
Far away, are the events of yesterday as night turn to day
And just for a little longer, no signs of the trials of tomorrow.

Rosetta Stone

A LONG DRAWN GAME

The balcony got silky darkness,
New phase of the moon
Not far from us - waves!
An anchored boat waits alone.

'So many days have gone
So many years!'
A long drawn game
Now we reach each other.
I could see her eyes in darkness
Once I saw them in trembling grass.

My lamentation echoed back to me
Does she hear the lament
Or the rupturous roaring sea?

A sigh breaks the silence
She chokes on words
I could feel her tearful eyes
Once I gazed at them under moon and stars.

The dawn breaks upon the window
Curtains are mast
The face in darkness has disappeared.

A blue page from a notepad
Its rough hasty edge
How calmly it says
'Please do not forget to
Open the oven.
Your basmati rice and roast chicken . . .'
And then some obscure doodles.

Saleha Chowdhury

BEAUTY IN BIRDSONG
(Dedicated to A M L Barnet)

A tiny bird has left the nest
And faltered to the ground
Her innocence is obvious
As she explores a new surround.
A happy stance, a singing call
With new ventures all around
But danger lurks
A cats' eyes search
But confidence abounds.

With loving care, the parents stare
Encouraging the young
A look out, and a special song
And a wing stretch just the one.
Launching on a wind swept breeze
And warmed by the rising sun
Unsteady on her first flight
With wings and air in fight
A little life has won.

To rise above the tree lined paths
Then circle the southern sky
And raise her own small family
And teach them how to fly.
When her life is near its end
She asked no reasons why
Again she flutters to the land
And shares a welcomed rest with man
To close her tiring eyes.

Barrie W Neate

PICA PICA

One day a baby magpie was brought here by a friend:
His wing was badly broken, it plainly would not mend.
I picked him up so gently - he gave a fearful shriek,
I felt my index finger clamped tightly in his beak.
I tried to coax him nicely, but all to no avail,
He fastened on that finger until the tip went pale.
And then he threw his head back and from his throat did well,
A sound so harsh and hideous it might have come from Hell.

Would you believe that magpie is now our bosom friend?
But don't be led to thinking his ways he chose to mend.
Oh no! He is quite charmless, without a single grace;
He has a pushy manner and menacing black face.
He's raucous and bad tempered, and eats just like a hog,
He chases all the nice birds and aggravates the dog.
His appetite's voracious, he gobbles this and that,
But best of all are maggots all wriggling, white and fat.

He thinks he owns the garden, he thinks he owns the house,
He creeps in through the kitchen as quietly as a mouse.
And then he does his damnedest, pulls paper off the wall;
Steals trinkets from the bedroom, leaves markers in the hall.
At 5 o'clock each morning he sings a serenade -
A sound as sweet and soulful as gravel on a spade.
So why then take a house-guest with manners that appal?
Well, that rude, naughty magpie has somehow won us all.

Jo Young

THE LITTLE GREEN BOOK

A poetry book of smallest size
Given gently by her hand,
Was to me a great surprise
For the gift was quite unplanned.

Much loved, this book was all to her,
She possessed no wealth or treasure,
But this, her fathers, she had kept,
Its worth was beyond measure.

Her life was not the easiest,
Two wars caused many tears
And in-between, few sunny skies
Would brighten leaden years.

But through all this the small green book,
Her link with father dear
Was hidden in an unseen nook,
Its loss her greatest fear.

Now as old age crept up on her,
She knew what she must do.
She gave my grandpa's book to me
Knowing I would love it too.

I promised I would pass it on
So the family down the years
Would treasure it as she had done
Through happiness and tears.

For this green book of little worth
In monetary terms
Has the fingerprints on every page
Of love, as each leaf turns.

Paddy Jupp

THE INTERVIEW

Howling winds surrounded the corner house
Embracing the wall's protective layer.
Inside, flickering candlelight
Reflected my face in the mirror,
As I rustled among long neglected letters,
In the antique dresser's drawer.
My eye reacted, drawn to your scrawled handwriting.
The memories surfaced.
It seemed only yesterday,
That I heard that fateful rapping,
On the old oak door, number 44.
Once again I relived turning the key
Remembering your tallness, enveloping me
Draining my soul at first glance,
Love at first sight they say.
Then the interview,
Sweet and brief.
Psychic experiences are all the rage
Your editorial knowledge,
Gleans my spirit,
Promises are made, of payment never received,
A centre newspaper spread.
A photograph, posed with fringed black hair,
Eyes promising untold mysteries,
Of paranormal experiences, and love.
Antique clocks surrounding the room
Have ticked away the years
As spiders silently weave, among paper cutting,
And love letters.
The corner house still echoes memories
Of Eros rapping at number 44.

Patricia Gargan

AT MIDNIGHT

The sounds are different at midnight,
Like the sounds of desires that reveal.
They are clearer, clean white, even ghostly,
Disembodied and ethereal, more real.

I awakened when I heard an orchestra begin.
The music flowing, sailing down the hallway,
Poured into the darkness of my bed
And raised me up to fall upon me,
Stream over me, enfold me
As crystal freshness, clarity and radiance
Of a splashing, gently crashing, waterfall.
Then as the curtains billowed in night breeze,
I heard *the voice* come smoothly singing,
Deliberately enunciating each word,
Falling in love again,
And I opened my eyes to calling, lovingly spoken caress,
Precious, sweet desire like dreams fulfilled.
I ran toward the sound for she was there,
Ran down the corridor, to the music, to her.
Liquid lights danced in green display,
Swaying with music floating through speakers.
A faulty timer! The spell came undone.
I pushed the switch and sank in my chair,
Silent as dark again, not even in dream.

Oh, the words and the music at midnight
Are the sounds of desires they reveal,
And, as long as I still fall in love again,
Sounds at midnight are different, more real.

Edgar Wyatt Stephens

ALARMED

An horrific noise, ten foghorns loud,
  Screamed crystal pitch, like a chimpanzee crowd,
My hand leapt out of bed, an automated reaction,
  Like a well oiled piston, from some steam driven traction.

My hand hit its target, with atomic precision,
  The alarm clock was silenced, its cries overridden,
How dare the alarm, cut incisive my slumber!
  My brain now activated, my mood black as thunder.

My dream had been interesting, though nightmarish at times,
  It was about walking up cliffs, with impossible inclines!
My eyes still closed, and feeling quite dazed,
  I rubbed them in a stupor, like windscreen wipers crazed.

I slowly hoisted my eyelids, like some mainsail rigging,
  Mining my energy reserves, with deep deep digging,
My head got out first, my body followed soon after,
  I descended as a heap on the floor, but I was in no mood for laughter.

I scrambled into my school uniform, never a pleasant task,
  I tried to assemble a serious expression; my intellectual mask,
I groped for the stairs and held firm the rail,
  Hoping my body would respond; I was feeling quite pale.

I got as far as the breakfast table, to my great surprise,
  Avoiding questioning glances, averting my eyes,
I noticed my mum smugly smiling, as my cereal disappeared,
  A small smile from my mum, is a look to be feared!

'Well . . . things have changed a lot since my day . . .
  I never used to go to school on a Sunday!' she said,
My hollow skull did a chameleon search of the rainbow,
  Eventually deciding on bright red,
I reached embarrassingly for the banisters . . .
  I yearned for a womb like refuge . . . a hiding place . . . *my bed!*

Clive Blake

UPRISING

A long time ago but
Remembered still
Somewhere upon a distant hill
A drumbeat sounds and the
Air around goes very still

Strange men appear dressed
In buffalo hides and feathers
With long bows on their backs
Leading ponies by their tethers
The war paint on their faces
Made them look like clowns from hell

No need to ask for whom
They toll the bell
They carry rifles or tomahawks in their
hands, and from their heads
Sprout feathers in tightly woven bands

Their courage would not desert them
In this clash with fate
Their arrows tipped with metal
And then well dipped in hate

They line the brow of the hill
In their thousands
The sun rises behind them
Like a large ball dipped in blood
They gazed down into a
Once fertile valley
But now no more than mud

The soldiers in the valley
Lift their heads
And shade their eyes
To see the moving tide
Of death to come

A cry like a wounded wolf in pain
Comes from the massed ranks
In front of the sun
As they charge down the hills
Together howling their war cry

The battle of Little Big Horn
Had begun

James Valentine Sullivan

THE PETULANT CHILD

We'd gone to Battersea Dog's Home to fetch an unwanted dog back
home, we had the love and care to give and were ready to have a pet of
our own.

So much choice, such heartbreak to see those dogs desperate for a small
sign that we'd welcome them into our home, though the day care would
be mine.

So I'd stipulated not a puppy, but a dog of two years old or more,
House trained, so we could form a bond that meant I could spend time
off the floor cleaning up puddles and other deposits that I wouldn't look
forward to sorting, so the family sat, the decision made firm before we
set out in the morning.

We walked along rows of cages, each housing an unwanted pet, a tear
in my eye as I wanted them all and knew it was only one we could get.
He squatted before a cage of pups, not more than ten weeks old.
'I want a puppy' came the wail from Harry who wouldn't be told.
We'd discussed this for weeks before, the reasons I'd made clear,
this was said again and meant, that a dog was what we'd come for and
a dog was what we'd get.

His lip drooped and he dragged his feet as I pulled him from the cage,
to study all the mature dogs as he stamped his feet in rage.

The looks I got from strangers, how cruel to deny him his choice,
but he'd be out all day, not me, so I ignored the petulant voice.

Dave and Kirsty spotted a mongrel with eyes that melted their hearts,
His age was three, he looked at me and we rushed to the desk with our
money to part.

He bounced as we took him to the car, his excitement knew no bounds
as Harry followed, still looking back, with his feet dragging along on
the ground.

Of course, once we got home Harry came round, as the newly named
'Pickles' sat on his knees and we laughed in delight as he settled to
sleep in a new bed with consummate ease.

The next morning, bright and early, Harry took him out for a walk,
when they came back I said to sit down so we could have an important talk.
I explained gently why no pup but mature dog was what I'd rather,
Then softly admonished his petulance at the dog's home, after all he's
no child - he's their father.

Channon Cornwallis

PATH OF FIRE

The cleansing of events that would seem to offend!
And the amount of these is limitless, there is no end.
The mind we have, cannot see into the future,
A brain we are blessed with, it is our own built-in computer!
For some it works well, for others, it is their hell,
Oh! what a story we humans have to tell!
For we are homo sapiens, the leaders of planet Earth,
Was this the reason that our mothers did give birth?
We tread a path of fire with pitfalls and concern,
Searching for the standards we are taught that we can earn,
Witness be the landscapes, in the process, that we burn!
Then we scream with fire and thunder,
When on us these things do turn.
Oh yes! what a story we humans have to tell!
We have bred an age of young ones,
Their sole purpose is themselves,
Their selfish plight they see as right,
They look out for number one!
Whilst we look on and wonder,
When will the change come on?
So it is quite obvious to me you see,
We do not have a clue! Will we ever get some sense?
But we don't look for recompense, that, is classified past tense!
Oh yes! what a story we have to tell.
So will we be life's losers?
We've fought our war, we've paid our way,
And now, we've had our say!
But will we all survive as such,
To compliment the great new day?

Bah Kaffir

ROSIE, MY HIPPOPOTAMUS

Now Rosie hates puddles and loathes getting wet;
the sight of a cloud brings her out in a sweat.
If the sun goes in we have to take taxis
and bribe dear Rosie with hamburgers maxis
and thousands of chips. She's as round as a top.
if she goes on eating, she's sure to go pop!
It's clear there's a problem (I've no idea why);
She's got to have something to keep her feet dry.
So off we went shopping for Wellington boots,
but the shoe shop flunkies burst out into hoots.
They gathered around, all the better to stare;
each arrogant creep had his nose in the air.
They hummed and they ha'ad and they said 'It's a bore.
Two boots aren't enough, she will have to have four!
The lady's quite strange, she's not quite the norm:
she'd better lose weight and refashion her form.'
The manager came when he heard their refrain
and cast on poor Rosie a look of disdain:
'My friends, I'm afraid it is time to talk tough.
I doubt if a diet is answer enough;
a figure like this is really *déclassé*.
She could lose two legs with advantage, I'd say.
There's an excellent man who specialises
in cases of odd and unusual sizes!'
I saw Rosie blush and I yelled at the brutes
'We don't want your sneers or your Wellington boots!'
We found a way to get over the snag
by wrapping each foot in a carrier bag.
And now through the puddles she merrily sploshes,
her feet safely wrapped in plastic galoshes!

Nicki Cornwell

TOO LATE

She waited in vain for a letter
That her son was too busy to write
To cheer and comfort his mother
And brighten a dark winter's night.

A cry of joy she uttered
At a fancied step in the hall
But the longed for voice was silent
And no one answered her call.

She stood by the garden gate
And gazed down the dusty lane
Her heart was sad and weary
And her eyes were full of pain.

The cottage door is closed fast
Her son had come too late
His mother's gone to rest now
She could no longer wait.

Don't wait to write that letter
Just call her on the 'phone
And say those words she longs to hear
'Mother, I'm coming home.'

Genevieve Tuke

THE MESSAGE

Soaring above the grey rooftops,
A red flash in a pale blue sky,
He followed longingly , blinking not to cry
Aloud in grief. He'd follow its direction
As long as he had eyes to see.
If only he had eyes just like an eagle,
Far sighted! On its tail a message,
Tied, knotted in string, went with it.
It cleared a pylon, only just, and headed
Over cliffs where desperate souls hurl
Themselves till all their tragic life has ended
On the rocks below. Then it was gone.

Years later, when all has been forgotten,
And, a man, he raked through heavy, dusty tomes
Of old philosophy, a letter came.
Inside, what seemed to be a rag once red.
It bled across the ill-scrawled note
Which, barely legible, proclaimed a find:
'Returned, the same'

Diane Burrow

THE SCOTTISH HIGHLANDS

On a Scottish Highland tour I did go,
a quiet holiday, I thought it would be so,
but from the very start I met two really nice couples who
came from my original home town too.
They were genuine 'Lancashire folk'
who happily liked to laugh and joke.

Norma was very much like Mrs Merton who is on TV
and ran a cattery out in the countreé.
Fred, her husband was rather quiet - but very 'dry',
several times we got 'our wires crossed' and we laughed until I did cry!

Marion was a nice chatty little farmer's wife
with several grandchildren, who gave her a busy life.
Bob, her husband was very helpful and kind
and came to my rescue, with my camera, several times.

They adopted me kindly and put me on a 'lead'
so everywhere we went - I did happily heed!

Between high mountains and through glorious glens,
along winding roads by many lockes and fells
only to stop for tea and to dine,
the kindly driver took us right to the door each time.
There was little time to buy, when we visited a 'gift' shop
before someone would call - we are off - you can't stop!

Across the new bridge to the Isle of Skye we did get
but true to tradition, it was misty and wet.
Up Ratagan Mountain, 1500 ft high we were told,
almost vertical it was, we prayed the brakes would hold!
The coach seemed to stand on end - but we reached the top.
The view was magnificent, and there for awhile, to take photos we did
                                                                    stop.
Oh dear! We then had to go down, the view was so lovely we nearly
                                                                    forgot.

Each evening we leisurely did dine,
the food was superb and then we chatted over a glass of wine.
Tomorrow we will have to rise at dawn, with a moan,
to leave the beautiful mountains and be on our way home.

Edna Parrington

DADDY

He came home from war
weary and sore
to his wife and two fine boys
but his money she'd spent
on pleasure hell bent
he left her and all her fine joys

Thirty-two years old
in business brave and bold
a secretary he employed
she was sweet sixteen
strawberry hair that gleamed
he fell in love, over the moon overjoy'd

When she was eighteen
off to Gretna Green
then a cottage by the seaside
two years later it was born
scapegoat Capricorn
who stole the attention of his bride

For the rest of his life
he gave the child strife
many times was she driven from home
but no matter where she runs
father, husband, then her son
the anger never leaves her alone

Jacqueline Taylor

1939 - THE EXPLOSIVE LOVE

You took my hand - my heart stood still,
The love within me began to fill:
I felt a burning within my breast -
The love exploded and would not rest.

I see you in the stars at night,
I see you in the clouds by day.
How wonderful, darling, to be with you
Although the times are far and few.

Whatever happens I know you're there,
And know you're thinking of me, and care.
My love will last - I love you so,
And please don't ever let me go.

Violet Impey

FORGIVE ME

Forgive me for what I have done,
My thoughts were only for me,
No thought of hurting others,
I just wanted to be free.

Free from all the confusion,
Free from all the pain,
For I went to the depths of despair,
Never to return again.

I tried all that was available,
But life was dragging me down,
In the depths of darkness,
No light for me was found.

I know friends and family,
Were always on my side,
I know all the worry that I caused,
And the things I used to hide.

Thank you for all the love and care,
I am sorry I caused you pain,
But now the clouds of confusion have lifted,
And I see more clearly again.

God bless all who love me,
For it's that love that gave me hope,
I have found a new life,
In a world where I can cope.

Now is the time to study,
To search until I find,
The answers to my questions,
That gives me peace of mind.

I know that I have found it,
For my mind is now clear and bright,
Please to help me recover,
By sending all your prayers tonight.

M G Bradshaw

THE SWANS

I saw two swans, majestic, white,
    upon a mirrored lake.
I saw them by the morning light,
    when I was half awake.
They sailed upon the water, clear,
    washed pink by rising sun,
The water was so silky smooth,
    as day had just begun.

The mirror image was so sharp,
    the trees upon the bank;
Though upside down, were like a park,
    where elves and fairies drank.
The swans, their wings of glistening white,
    arched up to form a nest.
Where cygnets, five; oh what a sight,
    rode where none could molest.

I was enchanted by the sight,
    I could have watched for hours.
The lake so calm by morning light,
    the banks bedecked with flowers.
It was indeed a fairyland,
    and only in my mind.
But I detect a master hand,
    who the whole world designed.

W Wallace McIntyre

GRANDAD: TRILOGY PART 1 - 120°

Strolling through the valley of recollection
I came across my Grandad.
When I was small he lived with us,
A lovely big house
Full of happy memories
Still standing - now home to strangers.
Strong character my grandfather,
Alone for much of his life,
I never knew my gran - died young you see.
But Gramp was always there!
He shopped for himself
Sometimes he would take me
To see the 'rushing waters'
And enjoy his glass of cider at the club.
Patiently I waited, as he scanned his paper
A great one for news and current affairs
He taught me much, without me realising.
In 1952 I joined the Army,
Never to see him again.
Suddenly in February '53 - he was gone.
I treasure his last letter I received,
But sadly never said goodbye!

T G Bloodworth

REQUIEM

The band played 'Jerusalem' as 'Britannia' left the quay,
And 'Land of Hope and Glory' before she headed out to sea.
A relic and reminder, perhaps, of a past colonial wrong,
Forgiven not forgotten? When Britain left Hong Kong.

The heavens had been weeping throughout the momentous day.
Were they weeping tears of sorrow or washing sins away?
They wept at the last Governor's last poignant parting song
And on the weaving 'Dragon Men' - when Britain left Hong Kong.

Some say the mystic dragon from the dark hills of Kowloon
Conjured up the tropical tempest on that fateful afternoon
To chastise the 'Foreign Devils' and show the waiting throng
That the omens were propitious - as Britain left Hong Kong.

Created from a small island in the Southern China Sea,
Britain leaves behind a city state, prosperous and free,
And the tearful past Governor prayed for that freedom to live long,
Supported by a rain-soaked Prince - when Britain left Hong Kong.

Also given to the enclave were a set of equal laws,
An international language and an impartial police force,
A non-political Civil Service of antecedents strong.
Will these all be jeopardised - as Britain leaves Hong Kong?

What will happen to the many who illegally crossed the border?
Will they be well treated by the newly nascent order?
Or suffer like the 'boat people' who fled from the Vietcong
And were rudely repatriated - before Britain left Hong Kong.

The band played 'Rule Britannia' as the Royal yacht left the quay,
'Now is the Hour' and 'Auld Lang Syne' as she headed out to sea,
Leaving behind an 'Imperial Jewel' and concluding the swan-song
Of a world-wide waning Empire - as Britain left Hong Kong.

William Wood

THE TALE OF FATHER FOSDYKE

The Reverend Fosdyke was so highbrow
The congregation raised an eyebrow
As he preached for endless hours
On divine principles and powers
Fosdyke was so frightfully boring
The people sat in their pews snoring
But Reverend Fosdyke really knew
The people snoozed within their pew.
One day as Father Fosdyke spake
A miracle made them awake
The congregation in their pew
Were stuck-up with heavenly superglue
Not knowing of the divine culprit
Father Fosdyke in his pulpit.
Now Father Fosdyke collapsed in laughter
And in the vestry died soon after
But never let it e'er be said
The sticky situation led
To writing on his epitaph:
'The vicar had the final laugh'.

Linda French

SPRINGTIME LAMB

We took a walk in springtime
Along the Derwent shore
Unknowing then the pure delight
That nature had in store

In a lakeside field
A pregnant ewe quiet and lonely lay
Not resting like the others
This was to be her day

She panted short and heavy
As she lay upon her side
Patient in her labour
From time to time she cried

One last heave and a tiny head
Saw the light of day
Very soon a little lamb
Was born and quietly lay

The mother cleaned her off-spring
And nuzzled it with love
From time to time to make it stand
She gave a gentle shove

There was a sense of wonder
To see a new life's dawn
We witnessed there a miracle
When this springtime lamb was born

Ray Ryan

MUMMY AND DADDY

(Megan and Jamie, born the 29th January 1999)

It all began late afternoon, we knew that we'd be with you soon.
We both decided that we were squashed and we'd get out,
no matter what the cost.
You know that pain down below, the one that hurt and wouldn't go.
That was us, we had to say. Watch out mummy, we're on our way.

By tea time we'd had enough, we want to move but it's just too tough.
So sorry mummy, we hurt you again, we didn't want to cause you pain.
It's the only way we could let you know. Come on mummy it's time
to go. Off in a taxi, we all sped. Poor old daddy looked fit for bed.

Drop Louise at Aunty Lynn's, not forgetting all her things.
We saw you daddy when you nearly fell, but don't you worry,
we won't tell.
We'll tell the nurses those glassy eyes, isn't beer, but just surprise.
We weren't supposed to come today. but bugger that we're on our way.

You worked so hard to get us here, all the pain and all the fear.
It was Megan's fault, she wouldn't come, so I had to shove her
with my bum.
But then before I could turn around, Kerry told you to push me down.
So I'm sorry mummy I came that way and with a cut you had to pay.

I'm sorry I gave you that scare and had to go to special care.
Don't you worry, we're both okay and now we're here
we think we'll stay.
So here's a poem from Megan and me, we hope we're all you hoped
we'd be.
To Mummy and Daddy, lots of love,
Megan and Jamie.

Lynn Brown

MEMORIES

There are things I'll always remember of days long ago
When walking on holiday on the river bank
Watching fish swimming to and fro
Lovely sunny, lazy days
Spent walking through the woods
Enjoying primrose and bluebells
The blossom coming into bud
Playing ball on the sands
Dad always ready for a game
I loved to run around with him
But now families aren't the same
We found so much pleasure in simple things
Money was short, it didn't matter
There was always so much to do
Such as listening to the birds chatter
We didn't sit and watch TV
But the wireless was always playing
Lovely music, exciting plays
The news to hear how the war was going
No ,we learned to sew and knit together
I made little dolls from the top of Mam's stockings
Made their hair from wool long and short
Until my friend came knocking
Then out to play what a time we had
Hide and seek, whip and top and skipping
At night we wore an old sheet
We were ghosts, round corners nipping
Oh yes, those days I remember well
Best loved, I often recall
Warm in my heart, bringing tears
Of lost days enjoyed by all.

Alma Taylor

A Neighbour's Warning

Of course I knew the facts of life,
But when about to become a wife,
A neighbour who wished she'd never wed,
Thought to warn of the perils in bed.
Her words to me she did not mince,
And as a girl they made me wince,
I must have been a little prude,
But her warning seemed so rude.
Since then I've chuckled many a time,
And just for fun put her words to rhyme.

When you're in bed awaiting sleep,
A groping hand begins to creep,
Along your leg and around your bum,
Then it wanders to your tum,
Up the rounded path it goes,
It's not searching for your nose,
Over bosom at dawdling pace,
It touches neck but not your face,
Bothering not with cheek or mouth
It turns away and heads back south.
First your chest and shoulder smooth,
Then down your arm it starts to move.
Across your hip and then it's there,
The groping hand is you know where!

To her it was a wife's worst chore,
She'd rather scrub the kitchen floor.
Poor old dear what would she say,
It she were in this world today?

Avis Ciceri

THE DRIVING LESSON

As I sat behind the wheel
and listened to the patient teacher
who talked me through, to touch and feel
'Be strong' he said 'the car won't eat yer!'

So off I went with a leap and a bound
to learn to drive in a country lane
We'll turn this corner and then go round
into this village he said with pain

I'll take you through a three point turn
forward and back then turn around
Watch and listen or you'll never learn
as the wheels churned up the muddy ground

Now stop here by the rippling pond
to let this string of horses pass
The car and I, we didn't bond
we joined the ducks en masse

No shouts or screams or tearing hair
he sat and stared towards the grass
And said he would be just and fair
but all I said was 'Will I pass?'

Isobel Clanfield

THE SEA VOICE

Picking up my cone shaped shell
I now telephone the sea!
'Hello Sea Voice, will you tell
What colour you wear today?'
She says: 'Neither blue nor grey
But in silver I still sway
With white foamy frills that edge
Those dancing waves you might sketch!'

'Sea Voice are you still there?
Is it true what they say
That winged waves when at play
Can be moon-dragged away?'
The Sea Voice murmurs: 'Hush!
Grown-ups' tales make me blush!
Why tie the moon to tides?
In such myths the truth hides!'

'Give me some mermaid news!'
The Sea Voice in my shell
Had one secret to tell:
At times mermaids dive deep
Pulling pearl plugs that keep
The sea from going down.
Now grown-ups will soon know
Why tides can dip so low.

Colette Thomson

THE TURKEY COCK

'Tis not a bird of which I write,
But of a public house, the home owned by our
Family long ago.
In a little village square,
In Hunsdon Hertfordshire.

Where cottages with flowers surround.
No carpets covered floors so clean
Scrubbed each morning floorboards bare
Cooking, cleaning day and night.
Linen boiled to blue bag white.

Not a car drove through these streets.
Horse and cart heaped full of hay,
Children skipped and hopscotch played.
Fields of buttercups and daisies,
Hedgerows covered with wild roses.
Haystacks we would romp all day
Surrounding woods of bluebells there to gather
In a life so far away.

The Turkey Cock no longer stands.
A runway laid for planes to land,
Came a second war another decade
All peace then was shattered.
Planes shot down and bombs were scattered.

Six years passed then life was normal
And the village still remained.

Childhood dreams still linger there
Of a life in far off days
In another time, another place.

Margaret H Mustoe

New Home: Arriving

They talked about the hill, to my surprise,
I thought, what hill? There's just a gentle rise;
I need not stop to scan the distant view
As breathless streets in Devon made me do.

So getting here does not take very long,
And then I'm greeted with such bursts of song
Of birds, as never heard in years,
The sounds of childhood sweet upon my ears.

Though near to town it's quiet and leafy green,
With lawns and modest plantings to be seen,
The steam-train railway runs along below,
Its sound so muffled that you'd hardly know.

Those living here may use a private gate,
A short cut to their church if running late,
But more, to leave the town itself behind
And walk in paths of quite a different kind.

The flat is now exactly what I need,
A sheltered base to fit the life I lead.
Church, shops and buses are not far away,
I'm settled here and this is where I'll stay.

Nora Martin

WHEN ELIZABETH RULED OVER ENGLAND

When Elizabeth ruled over England
The Catholics were her main foe
For it meant that the Catholics of Europe
Could deal England a terrible blow.

So she took land from prominent rebels
And gave Protestant royalists a share
Believing she'd solved her big problem
But things did not really stop there.

Quite rightly the Catholics were angry
How dare these folk steal all their land?
So they took up their poles and muskets
And thus as one - they made a big stand.

Then came one called Oliver Cromwell
The year sixteen hundred four nine
He chose towns Dromega and Wrexford
To make Catholic folk 'toe the line.'

He slaughtered the Catholic rebels
Not once did that man spare a life
Then he plundered the land all around him
Till the Irish felt nothing but strife.

The rebellion at last it was over
But the Catholics never forgave
Even now they are plotting and fighting
Though for some it must end in the grave.

Carol Turner

THE ARREST

Rain is falling, the night is dark,
A pool of light reflects a dancing figure,
Outside a house, two cars are parked,
A crowd of people steadily grows bigger.
A sobbing child, a struggling man,
A piping voice upraised in bitter protest,
'Don't take my daddy,' yet they can . . .
The man, the only object of laws' interest.

What did he do? What crime commit?
That vengeance finds the need to hurt his children,
Will time erase, will it permit
This memory to leave the young mind open?

It cannot be, it must live on,
And it will surely mar the childhood thoughts,
The infant dreams it has will all be gone,
Together with the good things it was taught.

Pat Church

MY STRUGGLE

Holy Spirit in my soul,
Shine your light and make me whole
Spiritually I want to grow
Give me faith, let your spirit flow.
I want to measure up, to your word,
My ears are open to what I've heard,
let me grasp that you're at work in me,
Water me, Lord, as you do a tree
Make me grow even stronger
I'm battle scarred, I won't last much longer.
Engaged in spiritual warfare each day.
Help me, Lord, it's to you I pray.
The devil tells me, I am hell bound.
In me he said, too many sins are found.
Although I stumble, bring me back.
I try to be humble, in the way I act.
Maybe I'm in a storm right now.
I won't panic, for I know your power.
Putting down deep, my spiritual roots,
My armour on, and my boots.
The weaknesses I am feeling, it's a struggle
Come Lord Jesus, give me a cuddle.
Christ Jesus, I have a hunger for you.
Will you be with me, and see me through?
This ongoing battle, I resist by faith,
Stumbling alone, yet I know I am safe.
Holding on to your covenant power,
I hope I am growing, just like a flower.

Sylvia M Harbert

WHAT IS LOVE?

Love is born in one, like a dream come true.
There are so many ways that love comes shining through.
So let's start with a baby, no let's start before;
We know it's love that creates, and need probe no more.
Creation no mystery, so let's pass on.
Think of the love a baby receives, especially the first one.
Its soft smile, the first laugh that's shown on its face.
That's love at the start, so let's move on apace.
It's then a child is so happy, they have no fears,
It's a mother's love that they seek when they first shed tears.
Now when school starts, it's then a new love is found.
It's not just in one place, no it's all around.
Then smiles turn to love, in their childish way.
It's soon boy turns to girl and love starts to sway.
From one to the other, until true love is found.
Then their love makes a new life, it's a merry-go-round.
He loves her today, she forgets him tomorrow,
Because their love is so fickle and can end up in sorrow.
But soon enough true love will be with them to stay,
We all hope that love will last for ever and a day.
So then they get married, and both plight their love,
To God in His heaven, who looks down from above.
And love goes on, through each day and each year,
It's then love plays a great part, when one sheds a tear.
And when the time comes to say goodbye for all times,
Love is there, shown in our hearts, and it's then that love chimes.
'Love is the greatest thing, the oldest, yet the latest thing,
We only hope that fate will bring love's story to you.'

Arthur E Holmes

A LIFE HEREAFTER

My two little grandsons came to stay
And we had shared such a lovely day,
When, I saw from the corner of my eye
That a baby bird on the ground did lie.

A more beautiful creature you never did see,
But our cat was staring, with a look of glee,
At the bird he had brought as a present for us,
And he wondered why we were making a fuss.

But the damaged bird was still alive
And to save its life we had to strive.
We laid it on a bed of moss
And, with our cat, tried not to be cross.

Although we found worms for it to feed,
It was mum that the little bird did need.
We tried to get water into its beak
But the poor little creature was very weak.

Our grandsons were willing the bird to live
But, by now, it had nothing left to give,
Although it survived throughout the night,
By morning, it had lost the fight.

The two little boys broke down and cried
And couldn't accept that the bird had died.
We made a casket and a cross
And consoled each other on our loss.

We all gathered round to say a prayer
And although we had all been full of despair,
I explained to the boys as we stood over the hole
We were burying the body but not the soul.

I told them that Heaven is a wonderful place
Where everyone has a smile on their face.
The sun always shines and there is no pain
And the little bird can fly free again.

Gillian Edge

THE THATCHED COTTAGE

The thatched cottage
      stood back in the lane
Its beauty I found
      hard to explain
There were flowers
      growing everywhere
The gardener had certainly
      taken great care
There were roses
      growing around the door
Hollyhocks, lupins,
      forget-me-nots, galore
The perfume of the flowers
      took my breath away
It was so lovely,
      but I couldn't stay.

I tapped on the
      white painted door
There was no reply
      so I went to explore.
Antique furniture,
      right down to the bed,
My nostrils could
      smell home-made bread.
Just a scatter of flour
      on the neat stone floor
Made it seem home,
      I wanted to see more.

Out in the garden
       a lady humming a tune
With concentration
       she did prune
She was a pretty lass
       dressed all in blue,
She suddenly tensed,
       so I took my cue
For a ghost like me
       would just disappear
So you see, she
       had nothing to fear.

Patricia Youngs

SPIRIT OF LOVE

Love that is hoarded only grows old,
You cannot keep it, or love will mould.
Love is no use until you impart,
Warmth that is living within your heart.
Be not loveless to your fellow man,
Convey affection as best you can.
A stony smile, it befits you not -
Take time to be friendly, find your slot.
Those who bring sunshine to other's lives,
Bring to themselves the same and they thrive.
Look out from the shadows, see man's need,
Love is the soul's health, to this I cede,
Love bonds together and avoids strife,
Parental affection is for life.
Delight in love that marriage holds dear,
Passion and desire over the years.
Now love first comes to us from above
Be not a soulless machine, but love.
We are voyagers upon this earth
Our duty is to love from our birth.

Ann Easton

MONSTERS

A morning mist hovers motionless just above the lake
dewdrops form as all around nature stirs to wake
in perfect peace and harmony, the dawn chorus adds its song
and sitting here all by myself - I quietly sing along

An invisible hand carries away the mist, sunbeams sift through the trees
with it all comes the smell of summer, fresh on a gentle breeze
Now with gauntlet thrown, challenge set, I am but well aware
I scan the water's surface, for any sign at all
there are monsters lurking - just out there

Not dragons, furry beasties or creatures from within a book
these monsters are beautiful, and to catch one you need a hook
then with a lot of understanding, patience to endure
frustrating hours of fishing bliss, and 'lady luck' upon the lure

The sky turns orange and all about other hopefuls pack up to go
peaceful day it has been, but the monster declined to show
the perch were hungry, the roach were too, with the bream most
                                        popular of the day
just one more cast, to be my last, before I head off on my way

Trap is set, my best cast yet, the lure comes flashing through the lake
line stops dead and turns around - a spectacular take
reel is screaming, line is singing, this is no hungry bream
rod bending in such a way, this is the monster of my dreams

Battle raging, war is on, this monster wants to win, he jumps and
                                        crashes to the surface
I've got to bring him in
One hour later, he gives up the fight, I almost did so too
this true tale of my monster I now tell to you
60lb he was in weight, I have never seen the like
as the applause echoed all around me, I kissed my monster pike

Malcolm Buckley

WAITING

I have waited for many an hour my love
As I sit on the golden sands
For your boat to return from the angry sea
So I can hold your hands.

And look into your deep blue eyes
As blue as the deep blue sky
Filled with your beautiful love for me
And I know they cannot lie.

You left me in the early dawn
Lying in my bed
You leant across and kissed me
But never a word was said.

And now I patiently wait my love
Waiting the whole day long
But my poor heart is filled with dread
For I heard the mermaid's song.

The mermaid's song brings death they say
A death far out to sea
I wait in fear and silently pray
Please God keep him safe for me.

I wish that I could be with you my love
In the depths of the cruel sea
But home I must go because I know
Our baby waits for me.

Jeanette L Durk

A WARTIME MEMORY

Sitting alone on a bench in the park
Watching the children at play
Running and jumping and laughing with glee
Making the most of the day

And as I sat there in the sun
Enjoying the happy scene
My thoughts turned back as they often did
To a memory that once had been

We were all so young all that time ago
What did we know of life?
Yes, there was war being fought overseas
But what did we know of its strife?

And then one day on a busy street
Being swept by the crowd along
I would have fallen when two strong arms
Lifted me from the throng

I looked into two sparkling eyes and a smile so disarming
A handsome soldier; bronzed and tall
And I thought 'Here's my Prince Charming

And so we flirted and played and had fun
Knowing we'd soon have to part
Came the day when he had gone
Leaving me with an aching heart

Months later I lay in the hospital ward
My eyes full of tears unshed
For my little baby had never breathed
And my handsome soldier was dead

As I walked home I couldn't weep
For no one knew my secret, the one that I would keep.

May Morrott

WHY I SHED A LITTLE TEAR

My mummy had a fall one day, she injured her poor leg,
She had to go to hospital, and was all propped up in bed.
I love my mummy very much, and I was feeling very sad,
She said I must look after things and help my dear old dad.

I have two little pussy cats, and I was caring for them too,
They kept me busy all the time, but what else could I do?
I cleaned up in the kitchen, and tidied up the lawn,
I then sat down and waited for tomorrow's dawn.

I said a prayer at bedtime, before I went to sleep,
And 'neath my pillow in the dark, I had a tiny weep.
Then in the morning Daddy called, he said that I should rise,
He had some news to cheer me up, it could be a nice surprise.

I was to stand at our cottage gate, and there was just a chance,
That I might see a vehicle stop, just like an ambulance.
I waited in the morning sun, and then at last it came,
Shining white with coloured stripes, and then I read its name.

Two men jumped out, and walking round, opened its large door,
And there sat Mummy in a chair, they wheeled it down the floor.
I had a great big cuddle, and a lovely smacking kiss,
She had now come home again, and granted last night's wish.

Daddy was so happy, and I'm sure the pussies know.
We will not let her fall again, we can't bear her to go.
Thank you Mr Poet for writing me these lines,
So Mummy knows we missed her, in her painful times.

Donald Futer

CHAPTERS IN THE LIFE OF A FAIRY TALE

It was an ill-omened day
ravens flew away
from me: why,
I now can see.

I succumbed to an easy death
dismembered bone from breath
blown on torment wind
madness was I sent

I met spiders in their lair
the bowels of forests where
they hoarded runes
most sacred

I escaped from their webs' keep
crawled through poisoned sleep
under the blood of earth
surviving as I could

I fought demons held them off
over mountain peaks aloft
borne on dragons' wings -
I heard the songs of kings

The woman lured me from doom
the darkness of her womb
taught me my
mortality

Sculpted me to birth
fire, sea, wind, earth -
a thing of light and sometimes
one of night

P Thompson

THE END

Behold the monster: hear it roar!
It's free and shall be evermore.
Those years it spent, growing in size
in a cramped cave, all now subside
beneath the weight of scaly feet
which crack the tarmac of the streets.
Like paper dolls, people tumble
from the buildings turned to rubble
as the beast passes slowly by,
its arms flailing from ground to sky.
First up high, it takes swipes at planes.
Then down low, it spits; in the rain
of mucus, people writhe and cry:
'Where'd this beast come from and for why?'
Then appears a bearded boffin,
so brainy he can't help scoffing:
'Don't you see? *You* made this creature!
For beneath its every feature
hang the ghosts of aborted lives
you'd sooner kill than let survive.
Every slight and each cutting jibe
you've ever uttered float inside.
Each time you looked away, more muck
formed within, adding to the bulk
of the beast now come to kill you,
crush you, flay you, rape you, slay you.'
The people look to him for help.
'There's none,' he said. Now hear them yelp
as the monster they made bears down,
breathes them in; in its lungs, they drown.

Richard Fallis

SPACE RACE

The medics had checked me,
       Condition - was peak!
I zipped up my spacesuit,
       'Twas tested - no leak!

My helmet was screwed down,
       I rose to my feet;
On entering the capsule,
       Was strapped to my seat!

The hatches were sealed,
       And the countdown began;
And soon perspiration,
       All round my neck ran!

The moment of *blast off!*
       Had come in a flash;
And gravity hit me,
       Just like a whip lash!

Then, all was sweet blackness,
       I fell in a swoon;
But soon I'd be first man,
       To land on the moon!

Ron Bissett

MUM'S TUMBLE

My mum's the best; she beats the rest.
She loves to live her life with zest.
When she got bored, her pride ignored
On shopping spree in BHS.

As she was sport for some adventure,
She mistook the escalator
For a slide and sneaked a ride
On an experimental roller coaster.

Though fit and nimble, she tripped and tumbled
And turned and tottered t'wards the floor.
She'd not been briefed about this 'beast'
So bounced and bumped on 'bot' so sore.

First aiders met her at the end
To patch and stitch her up again.
But she denied with pride all pain
And sauntered off to shop again.

The bumpy rumbly-tumbly jaunt
Has made her bum so numb and gaunt.
The numb is nearly not through use,
And in its place instead - a bruise!

Ruth Packer

CATS

Every animal has a mind of its own,
Especially Whiskers, who likes to walk alone.
You might think they are stand-offish, but they aren't, you know,
They are one of the first to cuddle up to you or be dressed in a bow.

A pussy does like to keep his own company a lot,
But in the quiet it's far easier to plot.
So just because they like to wander off by themselves,
Don't forget them and put them away on a shelf.

A pussy does truly love company,
But he also likes to feel free.
So give them love whene'er he should ask for it,
But never force it on him or he will do a flit.

Betty Green

NATASHA

Eighteen minutes to six in the morning,
Third of October the day was still dawning,
And while the whole world began stretching and yawning,
I was there at the birth of Natasha.

The midwife was Chinese her name was 'Nurse Ee',
She wrapped up the bundle and gave it to me,
And I stood and wondered at what was to be,
As I held in my arms my Natasha.

Then it was home and the world went quite mad,
I could not remember the life I once had,
All of a sudden I was known as a dad,
And I had a daughter, Natasha.

It was nappies and bottles and 2 am feeds,
Bath time and playtime and storybook reads,
A schedule so hectic I sank to my knees,
And all for the sake of Natasha.

She soon found her feet and toddled around,
Dragging a doll by its leg on the ground,
And all through the house was a wonderful sound
Of a life that was known as Natasha.

Then off to school full of sand, crayon and paint,
The fridge became covered in artwork so quaint,
A picture of Dad who she thought was a saint,
That's my little girl called Natasha.

After a time our lives went awry,
The marriage had ended and we had to cry,
But we both survived and I tell you no lie,
I made it because of Natasha.

So onward we went, 'The dynamic two',
A dad and his daughter the skipper and crew,
We found a new family and she loved them too,
A remarkable girl is Natasha.

And now here she stands at sweet seventeen,
A lovely young lady for all to be seen,
She's wearing my jumpers, in her eyes there's a gleam,
But I love her, my daughter, Natasha.

Paul Braithwaite

A Tea Shop Dream

Long ago a girl had a dream
To open a tea shop in a village somewhere
With pretty chintz curtains and oak tables and chairs
Tempting you in to sample her wares
Fine patterned china and tablecloths to match
All part of the plan for the tea shop she hatched
There would be all sorts of cakes, some fancy, some plain
And also meringues and chocolate eclairs.
Or how about scones served with cream and some jam
With a nice pot of tea, this was all part of her plan
But life turned out differently for this girl with this dream
She spent many years as a dental receptionist instead
And followed that by working in a lingerie shop
Till it came to the time she decided to stop
To retire and become a lady of leisure
And find other things to bring her pleasure
Such as dancing and knitting and helping others.
So although she never did get a tea shop
She is kept very busy quite a lot
Baking cakes for coffee mornings and fêtes
And to share with her neighbours
Who all enjoy the results of her labours.
Now that girl is an OAP
But enjoying life as happy as can be.
How do I know? Well, that girl is *me!*

Shirley Talmadge

THE LAZY CLOCK

Long ago in Fairyland there stood a fairy clock.
And all the folk in Fairyland obeyed its tick and tock.
It served them well for many hours, and also told of sun and showers.
Imagine then their great surprise, one day without warning,
It stopped, with neither when nor why, one morning at the dawning.
The fairy folk in great distress broadcast it on the wireless,
And advertised through *Fire and Loch.* (That's what they
                                    call the fairy paper.)
For anyone to mend the clock, to come as fast as they could caper.
So many came from far and near, elf and gnome and sprite,
Three goblins came with all their gear to put the clock to rights.
They peeped and peered and pondered and some just
                                    looked and wondered.
The clock just stood and smirked at them, and none could make
                                    it go again.
And then there came a lively sprite who prodded and poked
                                    with all his might.
And then he saw with some alarm, the fairy clock was sneering,
He took the elders by the arm and led them out of hearing.
'Now listen boys,' the sprite remarked, 'I think the clock's just lazy,
If you agree, I have a plan, 'twill need some thought, it's hazy.'
And so the sprite told them his plan, the others said 'You're crazy.'
But none the less they all agreed to give the plan a try,
And called upon Wee Willie Winkle around the town to cry.
So all night long Wee Willie crept and slipped through every lock,
While every elf and fairy slept, a dandelion clock.
Next day the clock was sad to see all interest in him cease,
He did not know that every elf each had his own timepiece.
And very soon the clock grew sick of always being ignored
And one fine day he gave a tick, and heard a soft applaud
The sprite stood at his feet and smiled. 'Come on, let's have another.'
The clock said 'Tick, tick-tock, tick-tock.' It wasn't worth the bother.
And now elves looking at the clock and dandelions round it,
Remember when it lost its tick, and the day it found it.

D Beaumont

WINGS OF A DAY

Summer in its drunkenness
Of thickened air
Shouted through the dawn
To a child unaware:
'Come, see life eclipsed in a day'
As the sun warmed the meadow
Of ripe ricks of hay.
The butterfly flitted
Through thistles and purple lush
Settled upon a blackberry bush
Sad because life today would close in,
The child again unaware watched with a grin.
Late summer afternoon of drowsy heat
Saw the child go home, weary to sleep
As evening's embryo of sunlit slant
Conspired with a river's remorseless chant,
Kingfisher shriek, mockingbird hum
Bore cruel connotations of a funeral drum.
Dusk's phosphorescence
Swept rays across fields
The blackberry bush is a pathetic shield;
Only a sinking sun witnessed the sight
And prayers of all creatures
Sifted through the night.

Mark Evans

WORKING TOGETHER

This little town of Rowell
Steeped in the history of a thousand years,
How well I know its homes, its lanes,
Its people's hopes and fears.
At the heart of England's rural past
Proud kindly folk lived here,
Concerned for each other's well or ill,
With neighbourly love sincere.
Some worked the land, and some with leather.
Life was a struggle before it began -
How was a family to be fed and clothed
On the meagre wages of a labouring man?
Poverty was all their lot - most could not read or write.
But intelligent they were and wise,
And in the 'Hungry Forties' planning together
They embarked on a daring enterprise.
It started with a sack of flour, some sugar, tea and rice
In Joseph Chandler's old back room.
The prices were low to whoever would join
And e'er long the sales began to boom.
The great plan grew and prospered well
Sharing the profit betwixt them all,
Till a few years on they took a small shop.
To one of them did the management fall.
A help with the food or a nest egg put by,
'This working together is good!' was their cry.
And fighting poverty in the extreme
They grew together in self esteem.
They were canny and wise in their generation,
Unconsciously part of a great changing nation.

Norah M Field

THE ADVENTURES OF SAM AND MR RAM - A DAY BY THE SEA

One glorious summer morning,
when the sun was beating down.
Young Sam and his friend Mr Ram,
went for a ride around.

They took off from the meadow,
into the clouds so high.
Sam astride the woolly fleece,
and down towards the bay.

The seagulls stared in wonder,
at Sam and Mr Ram.
As the happy pair descended,
to the warm and fluffy sand.

They both ate great big ice-creams,
as they strolled along the beach.
The gentle waves were slapping,
around Ram's cloven feet.

Suddenly! There was panic,
whatever had they seen?
A child upon a rubber bed,
was floating out to sea.

'Don't panic, lad,' cried Mr Ram,
as he ran into the waves.
Swimming strong against the tide,
he was so very brave.

The little child was crying,
the tears were running free.
When Mr Ram caught up with him,
his face lit up with glee.

'Jump upon my fleecy back,' said Ram.
'I'll soon get you ashore.
Your mother will be so relieved,
of that I'm very sure.'

All the crowd were happy,
that the child was safe and well.
They clapped and patted Mr Ram,
and his chest began to swell.

'That was a lovely day,' said Sam.
'It really was great fun.
I'd like to do it all again.
But please don't tell my mum.'

Alwyn James

OUR CHILDREN

Giving birth, a pain-filled joy!
Don't really mind if it's a girl or boy.
Baby's first smile, your heart takes a leap.
Your love for your infant becomes very deep.

Gurgling and dribbling, first tooth is due.
Many sleepless nights there could be for you!
Feeling proud when they say 'Mum' or 'Dad.'
Changing nappies, it's not so bad!

One minute they're toddlers with whom you can play.
But before you know it, it's their first school day!
Birthday parties they invite half the school!
Can't turn them away, must have them all!

Sports Day comes around every year.
Mums and dads will be there to cheer!
Then puberty's here in no time at all.
Boyfriends or girlfriends start to call!

Parents panic on their teenager's first date!
Watching the clock hoping they won't be in late!
Glue sniffing, drugs, becoming parents too soon!
We can't protect them from life, in a cocoon!

We just have to pray that the years will be kind
From troubles encountered we don't lose our minds!
School leaving time, exams won or lost.
Onto the dole heap we hope they're not tossed!

The years fly by, then they're married and gone!
You wish the best for your daughters and sons.
They present you with a grandchild then
All of your problems start over again!

Janet Dougherty

CULLODEN MOOR

Standing here with Charlie's men
Wanting to fight Cumberland's men
Listening to hear the shout 'Claymore'
Here on wild Culloden Moor

Now the fighting is about to start
We advance with braveness in our hearts
The English are using guns and more
Soon I will be dead on Culloden Moor

The English fill their guns from kegs
With grape, which only breaks our legs
The traitorous Campbells to the fore
Lead the way on Culloden Moor

Now Bonnie Charlie is away
Our kin find him places to stay
But in this place I'll stay evermore
For I am buried here on Culloden Moor

Katrina Holland

SUMMER MORN

Soft breeze and cool fresh air.
High on the hills we stand and stare
Beautiful the vistas on which to gaze.
Birds call and cattle graze.
Craggy rocks and gravel tracks.
Hikers travel with back packs.
Soft heather springs beneath their feet.
And farms nestle in valleys deep.
Clear, cold, bubbling streams,
Transformed by light of sunbeams.
Be still and listen, hardly a sound,
Just the crunch of boots on ground.
Peace and tranquillity all around.

Sheila A Waterhouse

A LESSON LEARNED - IN TIME

I thought money was important,
once upon a time.
It gave me such a feeling
that it led me into crime.
I could not have a best friend,
they meant not much to me.
Thought money in my pocket
was the bestest friend to me.
I wore designer garments,
'twas a shame I had no taste.
Now looking back in sorrow
and realise 'twas a waste.
I fell in love with money
when as a child deprived.
I then swore it would be rectified
and for acquisitions lied.
I could be bought quite easily,
thought everyone the same.
Bought presents for my neighbours
but a friend I did not gain.
Oh the years I've spent on squandering
gaining nowt but pain.
Have finally learnt a lesson
just before declared insane.
No rings now upon my fingers,
no more designer clothes.
I spent time amidst the grasslands
and have time to smell the rose.
Once I had a love of money,
thanks be to God it died.
Lord I'd like to love the way you love,
please plant that seed inside . . .

Rosie Hues

THE MINER

(Dedicated to my wife's father, 'Dickey' Swan, for the fifty-one years he worked down the pits.)

Fifty-one years down the pit
And what had Dick got to show for it?
A body full of scars, all healed up black
And lungs just hanging, like an old wet sack -

With a great set of mates
They would go down into hell
To dig up the coal that others would sell,
Flooding water, low ceilings and gas
It's a job, that I'm sure most of us would pass -

But Dick would go, with his tabs and his mates
And walk every day to the colliery gates.
To work on the face, digging up coal.
That was his job, his life, and his very soul -

Sitting in the chair, coughing up black
And describing to us, the pain so deep in his back.
His life down the pit had taken its toll
Fifty-one years of digging coal -

Dick and fellow miners kept Britain going
But they were stabbed in the back
Without them knowing.
The pits have all gone now, Dick as well
He's been released from the job that was hell -

A pick in hand and a candle for light
With only a canary to show danger and plight.
He would lead a pony, to dig on the face
To get to retirement was only God's grace -

At the age of fourteen, he first went down
Down in the ground, where there's hardly a sound.
Where the water drips and the coal seams creak
And out of the shadows the bogey man peeks -

He raised a family of which he was proud.
Roger, June and Thomas, his thoughts underground.
The Coal Board rewarded Dick for his caper
A certificate! Just a piece of paper!

John W Miles

THE LADYBIRD
(For Lauren and Ché)

A ladybird was once the source of much negotiation
By kings and queens and courtiers
Who would argue rank and station.

Do two spots make a captain?
And what of three or four?
Perhaps a major or a general
Or maybe even more.

'Pray do tell' they all enquired
Of the insect on the floor
They are but splashes on my overalls
From painting my front door.

John Forest Gaunt

THE BULLY

'I'm reading about that murder,' said Brian,
'I just can't believe it's true.
It's awful, really horrendous.
I wouldn't read it if I were you.'
'I already have,' said Brian's wife.
'It is such a terrible shame.
If you read a little further though,
You'll see someone else shares the blame.
The murderer was bullied as a schoolboy,
Just because he was quiet and small.
Apparently he was often kicked and punched.
He used to fear going into school.
He would lie awake and cry at night
Because everyone treated him so unkind.
No one could be unaffected by that,
It must have damaged his mind.
He must have been so lonely,
Feeling there was nowhere he could turn.
Maybe society creates its monsters,
There's a lesson here we can learn.
If the poor chap had never been bullied
Obviously this would not have occurred.'
All of a sudden Brian began vomiting
And could barely utter a word.
His wife ran swiftly towards him,
'What's wrong, love?' she asked helplessly.
'I've just seen the murderer's name,' he cried.
'It's all *my* fault, Jane. *I* was the bully.'

Colin Winfield

APRIL 1982

The enemy stormed the garrison
Took the military by surprise
But defiant Premier Thatcher
Sent a task force of considerable size

The fight to recover the Falklands
74 days in bleak terrain
The temperature sub-zero
Icy winds and pouring rain

The land invasion had started
Gunfire shattered the port
In the distance Stanley was burning
As the violent battle was fought

The *Hermes* and *Invincible*
With their protective screens
Of frigates and destroyers
Sought hostile submarines

An Exocet found its target
Amid shouts of 'Hit the deck.'
The *Sheffield* caught in an air attack
Was reduced to a smouldering wreck

Sir Galahad was sinking fast
Her casualties were high
The battle-scarred inferno
Was towed away to die.

Reclaiming of the settlements
Tumbledown, Longdon, Goose Green
by Royal Marines and Paras
Brave warriors defending the Queen

British counter-attack was swift
The brutal battle done
The silence overwhelming now
As the fight for the Falklands was won.

Hazel Smith

CHILDHOOD IDYLL

Childhood days - adventure days.
Will the sun shine - will it rain?
Will our mother let us play?
Will our best friend come to play?

With plans and schemes they set their sights.
Running and skipping with sheer delight.
Across the fields and over the hill,
Down to the stream which meanders still.

Quickly divest of socks and shoes,
Toes in cold water turn shades of blue.
Wading through stony waters - selecting
Strangely shaped pebbles for collecting.

Climbing the bank to lie in the grass
Short sips of lemonade to make it last.
Lunch unwrapped - a feast indeed
Swapping Madeira cake for seed.

An abundance of trees for climbing events,
The stoic oak with branches dense.
Nimble feet scramble its enveloping arms,
A fragrance of nature's foliage charms.

Then off to the woods where bluebells grow,
Through dark interiors bending low.
A shaft of sunlight reveals in glory,
Carpets of blue - like a fairy story.

Hot sticky hands clutch drooping flowers,
Dampened by the summer showers.
Home by seven - Mother advised,
Promise kept by obedient child.

Healthy outdoor occupations,
Children without reservations
Thrive - as Nature's garden shows,
A pattern of maturity grows.

Joy M Jordan

THE WORLD AND HIS WIFE

The world and his wife decided one day
To put man on this Earth to work and to play
They gave man legs to walk and to run
And hands that would please nearly everyone
Ears to hear and eyes to see
And knowledge awaiting just to be
A brain to think and a voice to say
And they made their pots from out of clay
For cloth they learnt how to weave
And to what he saw the world did cleave
All went well for a century or two
Then the human race wanted something new
It wasn't enough to sow and reap
They thought the world was theirs to keep
They needed a god of power and might
And each religion thought they were right
They killed their neighbours and fought their wars
Everyone believed they had a good cause
They invented the aeroplane, car and the shop
And nuclear power that none could stop
Now the world and his wife wail and mourn
And wish mankind had never been born

Sylvia Partridge

CRY OF THE HEART

Her heart cries out for love
A love so pure and true
Her being yearns for affection
Such that is real and sure

Oh the torment of a broken bride
Like the dark mist of the night
Oh what grief in a broken spirit
Like a wounded bird taken in flight

She looked to a future of love in bliss
With high hopes of promises received
All she sees is flickers of love in pieces
Disappointment in having being deceived

Oh the torment of a broken bride
Who glowed in love for her groom!
Oh the humiliation of shattered pride
That now makes her bow in gloom

She had given all her love
Until she became drained
What she asked was all his love
All she got was much pain

'How long will I bear?'
Is now the cry of her heart.

Jennifer Abdulazeez

MEMORIES

Once I was young and just like you
I ran and I danced the whole night through
But now you see me as old and wasted
Bones all bent and awry
Ears that fail to listen
And eyes that want to cry.
Footsteps that often falter
And memory that's nearly gone.
My fingers only fumble
When I want to get things done.
But try to cast your mind back
To just a few years ago
When *you* were only little
And 'twas me that had to bend low.
Remember the mountain climbing
And the fun of playing around
The parties and the picnics
Of hiding and waiting to be found.
The years passed away so quickly
I got old, but you grew as well
And if I really wanted
There's lots of funny tales I could tell.
But some things are best forgotten
And I would never reveal
Any of your little secrets
My lips I swore to seal.
One day in the distant future
I hope you too will be old
And think back to your dear old grannie
And never let on what you're told.

D Adams

MAD, MAD ENGLISH

The train pulled out, we watched it go
And what we said, you'd better not know.
It could have waited a minute more
Wouldn't have made much difference, that I'm sure.

The times we've stood in wind and rain
Only to find it's cancelled again!
For what we pay, the service is bad
To put up with it each day, we must be *mad!*

But just like sheep each day we're there
As in dirty carriages we sit and stare.
No one talks much, maybe a nod
Or even a grunt as on a foot they trod.

At Upminster for sure, they all pile in
Opening windows wide, and the cold to come in.
A curious breed the commuters are
Travelling up and down, from near and far.

Just once in a while you meet one who's nice
But you seldom see the same face twice.
Into London we separate, each rushing to start the day.
Then homeward bound, each of us
Ready to do battle, yet another day . . .

P Stennett

LIFE AND TIMES OF 'BOBBY'
OUR BORDER COLLIE

I'd chase you round the old settee; you'd scamper and jump full of glee!
With perfect ease you'd leap the stool!
Happy with our laughter, as you acted the fool.
At 6 pm you had your meal; how you knew time, you never did reveal.
Usually at 'News at Ten' a pot of tea I'd make,
But if I'd dozed off, you'd nudge me awake.
I'd wake with a start, with your head on my lap,
Or sometimes you'd just sit, and give a yap.
You'd have your biscuits and drink, enjoying supper with us, I think.
The call of 'walkies' almost drove you insane,
Excited at the thought of walking Hoot Lane.
In the woods, fetching far-flung sticks,
Never tiring, 'looping the loop' one of your tricks.
At Christmas time, you'd sit under the tree,
Thinking, 'Is there a present here, for me?'
As we unwrapped our gifts, we threw you the paper,
To rip and to chew, was a favourite caper.
Your gift from us, some tasty treats and toy,
You'd unwrap by yourself, you clever boy!
We'd had you as a cute wee pup from six weeks' old,
The love and trust you gave to us, worth more than pots of gold.
Your loyal and faithful company, we enjoyed for twelve good years,
And now you're gone, we cannot hide our tears.
But wonderful memories of you, we will treasure,
As through your life, you gave us such pleasure!
We knew we'd miss you, more than words could say,
As we said our goodbyes, on that sad grey day .
In time we'll smile, and will not weep,
When we think of you; in our garden, where you lie fast asleep.

Diana Margaret Barnes

CAT FLAP

Yesterday morning as I swung on my swing
Occasionally giving my new bell a good ring
I spotted a fat cat with huge saucer eyes
Smacking his lips as he swaggered close by.

I thought as I watched my foe clamber untiring
That being a budgie can be rather trying
Especially when stray cats pounce on a chair
With needle-sharp claws and paw my fresh air!

While I toyed with the notion of making my plea
Amid oceans of tears, on bended bird knees
My budgie-brain logic is put to the test
And calls reinforcements to disperse the pest!

As I squawked his name, old Rover came running
But cats as you know can be crafty and cunning
This one bounced off the chair disguised as a ball
Bowled over poor Rover then flew down the hall!

So today as I sit here on my little swing
Savouring the sound of my bell as it tings
Old Rover stays by me, guarding the hall
And practises catching a big furry ball!

Betty Lightfoot

A GARDEN TRAGEDY OR NATURE IN THE RAW

We watch the blackbird and his brown wife in June
Pecking with urgency on the dry lawn, for soon
We will be seeing them busy with their young brood
Who, clamouring noisily beg parents for food.
But horror! I find one black feather on the wind blowing.
I see the lone brown bird, feathers ruffled, wings drooping.
Not for the first time, our garden with fox scent is filled.
Last year, nestling wrens and thrushes he killed.
Cruel fox? Not so! He must see his young cubs grow,
To him the insect-eating birds were food providential,
Doing what comes natural, for his kind, is essential.

A Hall

PEDAL POWER

The tandem was polished, the tyre pressure's right.
The panniers were packed with our needs for that night.
The forecast was good, the sun's on its way -
We're going to ride over the ranges today.

We don't need an engine to get us up there.
We use pedal power - we're a dynamic pair.
The coaches and cars can speed by if they like.
We'd much rather be on our extended bike.

Mid-morning we're hungry and needing some food.
Did ever jam sandwiches taste quite so good?
Eaten by a stone wall, with sheep through the gate.
Then a swig from our bottles, 'Here's looking at you mate.'

At Rochester cafe we sat down for a while -
With tea and a scone all served with a smile.
Then time to move on, refreshed by our rest.
To put all of our powers of endurance to the test.

The ranges - well what can be said of this part
Of Northumberland, that county so close to our hearts?
Every climb was worthwhile, giving views by the score.
Breathtaking and awesome, and still there was more.

We dropped into the Upper Coquet Valley at last.
For that day at least the steep climbing was past.
Blue sky, rippling water, warm sun on our backs,
And only the occasional car rushing past.

Then into Alwinton, Clennell Hall, a hot bath.
An early evening stroll, and a chance to look back -
On a day to remember, a chance to review -
The joys to be found on a bike made for two.

Margaret Cockbain

THE MIRACLE

Clare and John happy, newly-wed pair,
Devoted to each other, walking on air.
Both working hard, to fulfil their dream,
To bring up a family, the best ever seen.

Their dream set in motion, first child arrived,
A son like his father, they were bursting with pride.
Truly this couple are above all blessed,
Baby girl born, God heard their request.

The children were thriving, life to all good,
But fate took a turn, John shed his blood.
Returning from work, he crashed on the way,
Never the same man, altered day by day.

He'd always been proud, an upstanding man,
Yet became a stranger thought his manhood was gone.
Clare tried hard to help him, it was not to be,
Their happiness seemed over, no future could she see.

Money was short, the bills were not paid,
John reached rock-bottom, his hope started to fade.
Then Clare had a shock, she was not feeling well,
Made a visit to doctor, now had something to tell.

Clare knelt before John, gently reached for his hand,
Told him her secret, of their baby not planned.
This miracle had come to pass, the family to save,
Born the lamb to show the lion now he must be brave.

Muriel Rodgers

HIS LETTER TODAY

It was an Autumn morn
When my son was born
I cried with joy
For my blue-eyed boy
Hence tender years
Such love and fears
First day at school
My heart was full
Secondary classes
How quickly time passes
University status
For him was the greatest
No sign of stress
With each glowing success
His future looked bright
And I thanked God that night
Though I knew in my heart
He was soon to depart
I heaved a deep sigh
At his gentle goodbye
To challenge the world
With his banner unfurled
It was on a spring morn, when my son was unborn
His letter today, said, 'Mother, I'm gay!'

Elizabeth Shirley

GLENCOE

The air is fresh at Loch Leven,
With mountains looming high,
The secrets hidden there within
Have long-since passed us by.

I hear soft voices singing,
The words about Glencoe,
I feel I'm drawn to stay awhile
And up the mountain go.

So we wend up mountain paths,
Wild breezes blowing past.
The sights to see not to forget
In our minds will last.

To see for miles great mountains tall
And in the glen below,
The shimmering lochs from the glorious sun,
Now gone. The winter's snow.

Now the rhododendrons
Their lilac flower endorse.
A sight to brighten many a heart
With the yellowing of the gorse.

There the mountains of the glen,
Stand high up in the sky.
Their secrets flowing in the mist,
Around the peaks so high.

So I travelled through Glencoe,
I feel I must return.
For it has such a lot to tell,
And I a lot to learn.

Beryl Smyter

TRUNCATED DEATH ROW FRIENDSHIP

Past the Florida, sunbathing, parasolled sand
There's a lonely death row prison cell man;
8125, his life on ice;
Thirteen waiting room years with no respite
From the battery hen cage, six foot by eight;
No family or friends in his nightmare wait.

As a young man he'd even tried to kill himself
But failed at this like everything else.
A no-good father left him at four
Stepfather and mother drank, abused him and swore.
Addict half-sister took her own life
Ray's body lived on but emotions died.

A bungled kidnap, an accomplice that lied;
Ray sentenced to four blank walls and to die.
His mother passed on leaving no one to write
Till a Berkshire school teacher's postcard arrived;
A drop of love in his loveless life
Thawing ' the frozen boy' inside.

Letters now criss-cross the ocean deep
So two distanced people a closeness keep;
Two people so different in every way
Yet a soldered connection, heart to heart, was made
Between Ray, the prisoner sentenced to die,
And Mary, who walks free in the Berkshire countryside.

The switch is pulled; his head snaps back,
Senses lock, mental fibres crack;
His body burns while an ember glows
Buried deep in the kernel of Mary's soul
And though his ashes scatter in Florida's sky
Ray still lives in the Berkshire countryside.

William Greig

WHO DUNNIT?

A youthful teacher faced the class
Her wisdom to impart.
These ten year-olds filled her with joy,
And teaching swelled her heart.

Creative writing was the task,
'Just write your very best.
Religion, life and mystery
The subjects for your test.'

With heads bowed down and pencils poised
The children they began
To fill the pages of their books
When Mary said, 'I'm done!'

'You can't have finished yet,' Miss said,
'Just carry on and write.'
But Mary said, 'I promise you,
I wrote with all my might!'

The teacher shook her head and said,
'All right, show me your wit.'
The girl read out, 'My God, I am
Pregnant now, who dunnit?'

Elizabeth Spencer

AGONISINGLY AMBIGUOUS

The gypsy spoke for a long time,
About The Water Carrier.
Out of the rain the woman sat, dishevelled.
Drained in yesterday's years; Listening,
To her patter, pouring, and lapping it all up.
Meddling she was in the mirrored memories
About to burst their banks,
And, finally, breaking them, until,
Infinity fused.
Electrified . . .

'Embrace the rainbow!'
'Now . . . How?'
'Take it back!'
'What?'
'The ring, round, eternalled and returned!'
My conscience sighed . . .
'You won't be missed!'
Kaleidoscoped,
Embraced we did.

The gypsy craved The Creed;
Aquarius bound,
Long winter fingers fed the cracking cards,
Like lashes, licking the skin off stunning truths.
'God makes mistakes my friend.'
She groaned about Golgothic grains harvesting in hell . . .
Eve-like I wondered at the world appearing.
Forgiven, fate, it fumbled for the tree that really knew.

Some opiated rhymes, threw up some lines.
Like Moses, standing confronted with his tentative *tablets*.
Stopping at ten?

A Tonner

CAMELOT

Across the bridge of golden hue,
Young knights and merchants, maids and youths.
A goodly number honest and true
Of fair townspeople trod the path.
And all to see this stranger new
Who'd travelled far through vale and heath.
An eager maid with years but few,
Who'd come with love to pledge a troth.

On hill they stopped as she rode by,
And each, with candle, glanced her face.
For thus they held their lights up high
And as she passed she slowed her pace.
Countenance pale and smiling, shy
She searched for eyes which began the chase.
And beyond the crowd she heard a sigh
And watched him, waiting, without haste.

Now smiles still smiling, each by other,
To Camelot they both are drawn.
Towards the lights like child and father,
A vision which radiates till dawn.
But one among the crowd does hover
With gallant thoughts of honour, torn.
For raging youth won't choose a lover
And such, on chastity, will pour scorn.

When like on like the eye doth dwell,
Then passion is ruler over care,
And marriage bells ring forth their knell.
So; Lancelot, Arthur and Guinevere.

A Higham

VANESSA

My journey home, my work complete,
A joy on motored bike!
Was soon to end and Far'del Street,
My joy and I alike.

It's not the pain that tortures me,
Nor blame, given to cause,
But time that passed laboriously,
Like life's great world did pause.

I ponder the time, I lay forlorn,
Darkness and mind in dream.
From out the void came the dawn,
Thanks due to a special team.

It is that team with special skills,
I owe, for given chance,
For me to fight, those painful hills,
Head high and now advance.

Sadness! That once filled my heart,
Replaced by love, not bile.
Bestowed on me, new dreams to start,
What better than with a smile?

You see! I'm given another chance
To see, when blind before.
My strength, my thoughts, I do enhance,
Into that void no more.

William Lea

PAUL?

On the way home from work one day, I stopped
By the paper shop to give a lift to a stack of boxes with legs.
It turned out to be a boy from up the road, called Paul.

'Whattya making Paul?' I asked.
'Time machine!' he replied.
I smiled and dropped him off outside his house.
'See ya!' he chirped.
'Yeah, see ya last week.' I smirked, driving on to my house.

A week or so later, I was frozen in my tracks by what I thought
was Evel Knievel's grandson pelting down the hill towards me!
In the seconds it took him to whiz past me, I realised it was Paul,
Off once again on his adventures, this time on his way to a karate
lesson; complete in suit and cycling helmet . . .

(What a guy, last week - rocket scientist, this week - dare devil!)

Now maybe it was just my imagination, or a trick of the light,
Or whatever, but I thought Paul actually looked that bit younger than he
had on our last encounter a week or so ago. Maybe he . . .
Maybe . . .
Maybe . . .
Paul . . .
Paul . . .?

Jared Pegler

THE BULLY

An angry face looks into space as people turn to stare,
I'm upset now, don't ask me how and you're just standing there!
You called me weak, a little freak and now it's plain to see,
That I am strong, you got it wrong, 'cos you're the one, not me!

You called me sad, now I am glad that you are now to blame.
The day you took my life away things never were the same.
You ridiculed and laughed at me, when I did nothing wrong.
You said, 'You'd better go away cos here you don't belong.'

I hope you're happy insecure 'cos I'm just fine and stable
You could come and apologise, I doubt that you are able.
So go away and live that way, just bullying and bluffing, and see what
people think of you . . .

The answer will be . . .

Nothing!

Sarah Williams

TRUE ADVENTURE - THE INFAMOUS FIVE

On the Norfolk Broads we decided to venture.
Four women, one man in a sailing boat
To cope with all this coming adventure
A book from the library, would help us to cope!
When we first saw the boat, it was a thirty footer
We nearly passed out, was this a joke?
But with sails up and all of a flutter
We really felt like navy folk.
Our luggage was mostly home-made wine,
With some food of course, on which to dine.
Mistakes we made, about one a second
By the end of our struggling the river beckoned,
On our first try-out, we were stuck in the mud,
But with some help came out with a tug
In between we had loads of laughs
Mostly at ourselves and all our gaffs.
A hurricane warning was given out.
So we asked the skipper to turn about.
He wouldn't tho' he had learned to tack
Was enjoying himself and wouldn't turn back,
So my mate and I sent him down below
With the other two girls who didn't want to go.
We bolted the hatch and locked them inside
Went back on the engine, to moor, riverside.
The skipper and girls had drank all the wine
They were all asleep, drunk out of their minds!
So wet and tired we had led a mutiny -
But we both missed out on the liquid booty.
It was a super break we wouldn't have missed
We were really proud we had tackled this.

Jean Dutfield

THE DOORMAT

He struck the unfortunate maiden
Whose innocence offered no shield
The kitchen floor caught her quite coldly
And witnessed the blood that congealed

His tongue made the sound of a whiplash
That all of her neighbours could hear
The menace it was that enraged him -
His over-indulgence in beer

Her eyes soon were swollen from crying
Whilst self-esteem lay torn to shreds
A pattern of boot marks upon her,
The doormat upon which he treads

He stumbled to bed fully clothed
And snored his way through to the morn
When, 'til the next time, he was sorry
With a well-practised look of forlorn.

Kim Montia

BLIZZARD

I hate to drive in pouring rain,
or blinding sun in blazing heat.
At night those headlights are a strain.
With bloody snow, I can't compete.

I recall well that certain time,
when I got lost in such a squall.
My engine had been running fine.
But with one cough it then did stall.

Without a clue where I was at.
I found myself banked in by snow.
No sign of life, I simply sat.
And panicked more than you could know.

So new to this, was not prepared,
with shovel or means to keep warm.
No phone, I felt completely scared,
with news of season's fiercest storm.

From encased windscreen peered a face.
My relief was easy to trace,

My saviour was local farmer,
who dug until he got me out.
I hugged my thanks and felt calmer.
Was told, 'Help is what life's about.'

'You'd be surprised the times there's need,
to rescue folks from winter storms.
I think that you should let us feed
and shelter, till the weather calms.'

I'll live my life in gratitude,
for farmer's hospitality.
Whenever now storm does intrude,
I think of my mortality.

Leslie Fine

A MURMURATION OF STARLINGS

Perched in rows on the garden fence
Like crotchets on a music score,
The starlings trilled their eloquence,
Black iridescent coats they wore.
Twittering in the cupressus
Their young so newly murmurous.

They chirruped gaily looking down
Playing games in the morning sun;
Knowing Cat was making a frown
Grimacing dissatisfaction,
They saw green glints within Cat's eye
Not knowing that a friend would die.

The cat moved quickly to the trees,
Expectant claws to branches clings.
Startled, the birds rose on the breeze
Blackening the sky with their wings.
Dark foliage around dark fur
Waiting, watchful beneath the stir.

The feline knew they would return
They always did to play their game.
A game Cat didn't have to learn;
Instinctively to sport he came.
The first black starlings perched once more,
Unaware of what lay in store.

The birds amassed and tauntingly
Heralded on the summer morn.
A furry flash leapt from the tree,
In its mouth a fledgling forlorn.
The baby shrilled and then was still,
The cat disappeared with its kill.

Susan Naile

THE PRIMARY SCHOOL CLASSROOM (1965)

Lightning flashed. All pupils were whipped awake.
Shiny arrows flew across the sky thick like candyfloss.
The voice was smothered in dumbstruck stillness.
The teacher was no Superman. He was frightened and cross.

The Alps closed in. Hannibal marched on plastered walls.
Death, bloodred, drowned in spoils of Roman wars.
Among the prize-winning water-colour paintings was mine.
Depicting a gory battle, where soldiers fight until they fall.

Tempus fugit. The old carob tree was like a hunchback.
It whispered something I couldn't catch, from the past.
I listened hard, but the breeze blew in gale-force winds.
And the tune changed from rock to rap and talking fast.

Years are fossilised like roots grappling with death.
I travelled, bought souvenirs to remind me of mystery:
Since I was born, men have been to the moon and back.
Suddenly it's the year 2000: the present becomes history.

Raymond Fenech

MATTHEW AND MATTIE

An old empty house on the edge of town stood
With windows and doors by the score,
But a secret it held in the bricks and the wood
For Sir Matthew he dwelt 'neath the floor.

Sir Matthew he was a large grey mouse,
With top hat, tails and a cane.
He strutted about round this old empty house;
To feel so important his aim.

Not far away was a field filled with wheat
With poppies that shone in the morn.
Down near the roots way out of the heat
Mattie, the field mouse, was born.

Mattie he was small, scruffy and brown
With baggy pants and a straw hat.
He scampered about and acted the clown
By teasing the old farmyard cat.

Mattie one day from his field of wheat strayed
To roam in the hedge near the road.
He ate berries and seeds and with other mice played,
Then stopped to admire a green toad.

The same day Sir Matthew went out from his house
And strolled down the rough cobbled lane.
He happened upon the toad and the mouse
Who were clearly enjoying a game.

So very soon after these mice and the toad
Had developed a friendship so true.
Their long summer days were spend at this abode
Playing leap-frog beneath skies of blue.

Sue Goodman

FIENDISH PLOT

With video machine that's new
Installed, we come to driving test.
The second part of thriller's due
At time we have to be away.
To fathom rules, to set the times
And channel three, it seems we need
At least a PhD in maths.
At length we fix the fiendish thing.

It's time to settle down to solve
The crime and who will win the girl.
' . . . unlike the present Government,
We will keep our promises. We
Propose . . .' It seems we've videoed
A party politician's drone.
With sound-bite insincerity
He grinds to his tedious close.

A message flashes on to screen
'All our programmes are running late
As semi-final match was forced
To run to extra time , . . regret . . .'
At last our thriller starts. The plot
Unfolds until we're on the verge
Of solving all. Adverts intervene,
As timer guillotines the end.

Henry Disney

THE FIVE AGES OF WOMAN

At the age of thirteen and a woman you've become
You think you know all there is to know
Up until you're twenty-one.

At twenty-one you realise that you really knew so little
But still you have a lot to learn
As you realise that life can be fickle.

When you reach the age of thirty-five and two children you have borne
You feel so great to be alive
And you sense that you've weathered the storm.

The next thing you know is that now you are fifty and life seems to be
passing you by
You think of your pension and start getting thrifty
And you're conscious that someday you'll die.

You've now reached the age of seventy-five and aware that you're now
all grown up
You look back on life with a knowing expression
So happy you're not still 'a pup'.

Eve Daily

WART A PITY

Once there was a Prince who had a wart upon his nose.
He fell in love when he espied the lovely Princess Rose.
He knew he'd never win her, but he told her he'd be true,
She only laughed at him and said, 'Goodbye and warts to you.'
The wart grew even bigger, it was shaped just like a horn.
It made him quite cross-eyed and wish he never had been born.
He went to all the doctors, 'Please help me now,' he said.
If I can't get this wart off, I might as well be dead.'
Alas, they could not help him, so he wandered far away.
When in a thick pine forest, he thought he'd like to stay.
He came upon a dark old hut beside a weed-choked ditch,
And living there inside the hut, he found a dark old witch.
She looked at him right carefully and said, 'It's very clear
You'll need a spell to help you. I've got a good one here.'
She mixed it and he drank it, without the slightest fuss,
It changed his shape and he became the first *rhinoceros*

And he lived clumsily ever after.

Margaret B Baguley

THE PRIZE

I know self praise should never be sung
But I won a few prizes when I was young
Books, a shield and medals as well
But my greatest prize was when I won Nell

As I came from the station she stood there
The sunlight gleamed on her raven hair
Her eyes were bright and honest without a hint of guile
And I saw the blush of shyness and her little half-formed smile
I too was shy and nervous as youngsters used to be
But I knew I had to ask if she would walk with me

We were young in the summer of 'forty-four'
Bang in the middle of Hitlers war
And now I had met the girl of my dreams
My squadron was posted overseas!

But in that fleeting desperate time
On parting I knew that she'd be mine
We pledged our love as I went to war
Knowing that if I came home once more
We would marry, Nell and me
And be as happy as we could be

It all worked out and happy we are
And I give all credit for it to her
She is patient, good and kind to me
And brought up our children so carefully
Our house is spotless and she cooks like a dream
You praise your woman - I've got the cream

What a wonderful treat I had in store
When I won first prize back in 'forty-four'.

David Merrifield

CROSS PURPOSES

Sunday morning

Dear Jan,

About our row last night - it's all
a big mistake. I couldn't live without
your love - forgive me if you can. I need
to see you right away - it shouldn't end
like this. I'm sorry for the things I said;
you mean the world to me. Please say you'll come - same time,
same place   (beneath the clock).

Love Tom

Sunday morning

Dear Tom,

About our row last night - I think
you're right - the end has come and we must part.
I've learned a lot from knowing you, but times
have changed and so have I. Perhaps, one day,
we'll meet again and know that what we did
was right. So, just for now, I'll say goodbye.
Don't write, don't phone (not even once).

From Jan.

Ellen Green Ashley

WHAT A MEMORY

Who was that teenager long, long ago?
I've a funny feeling I should know.
Dancing all night, and so carefree,
No, I cannot believe it, that wasn't me.

Then in her twenties, a marriage took place,
Looking at photos, I should know that face,
But there's no wrinkles and no grey hair,
Wish I remembered, it just isn't fair.

On to her thirties, and children three,
About their mother? I don't think it's me.
If only my memory was not such a mess,
I'd know what was what, and not have to guess.

She then entered her forties, give me a clue.
I'm trying so hard, I'm sure it's all true.
A silver wedding? You must remember.
Oh yes, of course, was it June or September?

Now in her fifties, with grandchildren playing,
What was her mother's favourite saying?
'If your memory's not good, and you're not really sure,
Just write it down, and it's there evermore.'

Then she was sixty, and things still a blur,
How come these events, (if they did occur)
Are so very difficult to recall?
Surely a few things, but not all.

So when she reached seventy, and looked back through the years,
She thought of her lifetime of laughter and tears.
Life's such a challenge, we all play the game.
Oh, now I remember that teenager's name.

Me!

Edna Tomes

BENGIE TABBY CAT'S ADVENTURE IN THE SNOW

Looking from his bedroom window, Bengie had a great surprise
Everywhere all covered in white, he couldn't believe his eyes
He had never seen snow before, his excitement rang far and wide
No time to waste as he rushed downstairs, he longed to be outside

His mother Tabatha was worried, with wet fur he might catch cold
Once again Bengie took no notice, he never would be told
He thought it was great fun, as he placed his paws in the snow
Meeting Cousin Rupert Black Cat, for more mischief they would go

Bengie was really fascinated, as more snow fell from the sky
Many were having snowball fights in the field as they passed by
Entering into the firing line, Bengie was hit by a snowball
He thought perhaps coming here, wasn't a good idea after all

Over by the river, Bengie spotted children building a snowman
He cried to Rupert let's go and see, we'll help them if we can
But they were more of a nuisance and were soon chased away
Meowing back they scampered along and both began to play

Then all at once Bengie slipped and fell down the river bank
Rupert couldn't see him anywhere, his heart suddenly sank
He then noticed Bengie sliding, on the river which was solid ice
Bengie called for Rupert to join him, as this was really nice

He slid right out towards the middle where the ice was very thin
Unable to hold his weight, it cracked and he fell in
Rupert didn't know what to do, there was nobody about
He must seek help before nightfall, there wasn't any doubt

In the distance he saw Farmer Jones with his dog named Rover
They heard Rupert's cry for help and both hurried over
Without hesitation the farmer sent Rover, down into the river
He took Bengie by the scruff of the neck and swam back to deliver
Safely back in his home, Tabatha thought he was lucky to survive
Bengie lay shivering with a chill but it was so good to be alive.

Linda Brown

ONE CHARITY THAT'S NOT CHARITABLE

Disabled people from far and near
You had better hold on, to things you hold most dear.
Several months ago
When life to me, had taken a low.
I joined a club, set up for the blind
It helped me immensely, to clear my mind,
I had never sung, in my life before
Until I arrived on Cornwall's shore.
A charity that's run for, the visually impaired
It was they who got my life ensnared.
Into a choir I joined, I sang in bass
My wife bought some ear plugs
'Well!' she said, 'That's just in case,
I have heard your attempts at singing before.'
Ah! But that was before I arrived on Cornwall's shore.
For years I wanted to join a choir
When you can't *see* to read music, it kills the desire.
But as the whole choir, were in the same boat
We all pulled together, that kept us afloat.
With concerts I had sung in, many under my belt
Was I the only person, who honestly felt
We needed a logo to promote the 'Blis' name?
'Blind in song' for me, they never remained the same.
After pricing the garments and lowering the fee
Many hours and months, had I wasted on thee.
When shove came to push, and time to decide
'Blis' got to their feet, and all went to hide.
A committee was called, trustees galore
Was it those, that I'd seen washed up on the shore?
Decisions were made, let's throw this man out
We can't have him present, he knows what it's about.
His head is enlarged, his nose is long too,
We'll withdraw his membership, that will make him feel blue.
Now, I've managed to turn, this poem around!
I've got off my chest and pulled myself off the ground.
A word of warning, to all folk who care

To people who donate money and hope to help share,
If you're going to give money, then pass this one by
Or you too might end like me, *blind, with mud in your eye!*

Les J Croft

MY MUM

Long, long go, in the last century
There was born a wee girl who was named Anne Marie.
As a child she was quiet, well-mannered and good
Although she was wilful she would never be rude.
She grew up to be a tall and an elegant teenager
Who could never resist a challenge or wager.
She left home to go to college to get a degree
Then set off from Ireland to sail across the sea.
When she landed in Spain she got a post as governess
To a girl called Mercedes who was a real-life countess.
The family lived in a castle so she felt like a queen
And she stayed for six years until the girl was eighteen.
As she sailed back to Ireland to her own family home
She planned where to go next as she still wanted to roam.
South America called so she obtained a visa
But Fate intervened in the shape of my Da.
She met a young man and knew he was her Mr Right,
As they both used to boast . . . it was love at first sight!
So they married six weeks later and now that she was a wife
She had to adapt to brand-new style of life,
The next year a baby was born to start their family
Then another two years later and then another . . . that was me!
As there were no jobs they emigrated across to Scotland
It was hard and the children were too young to understand.
Another baby was born to make their family complete
So Mum had to control her two 'itchy feet'.
Still she had a long life and was an example to everyone
And she died at the grand old age of ninety one.

Mary Anne Scott

WET SUNDAY

All of that day it rained
and the drain overflowed
drowning dank cadavers of leaves . . .

Too wet to go out walking far,
the car too gleaming clean,
they took a brief turn round the block
then ate their meal with Radio 4,
leaving the washing-up in soak
to sit in easy chairs with open books . . .

She saw his eyelids close, his head fall back,
she took the letter from her bag and read
it once again, feeling her pulse-beat quicken
with the living past and the present pain
turn in her like an unborn child
            - You remember X? - They found him dead,
            his heart . . . the stress . . . so very sad.

A heavy burst of hail
on the window pane,
she looked up startled,
saw his face as it had been
laughter-creasing through the blurred glass
of the many deeds and days gone . . .
She smiled and blew a kiss to him,
disappeared unshared time
- while her husband went on sleeping
through the incessant rain . . .

Kon Fraser

SACRE COEUR

She stands at the top of the steps, gazing down into her past.
The ghosts of her youth surrounding her, like dancers at a ball.
Tentatively touching, 'Oh remember me! Remember me!'
And the years peel away, swirling like autumn leaves in the wind.

The studio she shared with Jaques so many years ago.
Its smell, by day, oil paint and dust, at night became red wine and lust.
She passed enchanted days bewitched by love, and thought,
Stretched sensuously, on his dais, to be immortalised in art.

But the year moved round full circle, it was time for her to go,
And no, he didn't say, 'Please stay with me! Don't go!'
The innocence, the love was given freely on her part,
And she left with him the gift, of a small part of her heart.

Barbara Alcock

DRESS REHEARSAL

Oops! Don't laugh! Now then, dearie -
  Are your legs a little weary?
Can't help that - your *timing's* wrong -
  Perhaps it's your elastic's gone!

Come on, darling - never mind -
  I'm only trying to unwind
The tangled mess you've made of it -
  No! We can't stop for a bit?

Now, come along, love - that's not right -
  You're what? Your leotard's too tight?
Well, take it off . . . ah, 'Gawd', not *here*!
  Where then? Straight down the corridor
And then turn right - it's the third door -
  (Or is it fourth?) - I'm never sure . . .

I cannot take much more today . . .
  You 'goddam' tape recorder - *play!*
I've had enough! Must have a break -
  You lot - 'Take five' - don't come back late!

That's better, now - let's start again -
  Rely on me to tell you when
You're ready for the 'real live show -'
  I love you *all* - or didn't you *know?*

N Mary McCaig

THE MUSIC TEACHER'S TALE!

Dear Lady Blanche
I'm sorry to say
Your son has caused me displeasure today.
His attitude is not quite right.
His practice was not done last night.
I really think the violin
Is not the instrument for him.
His scherzos certainly don't compare
With those of your charming daughter, Clare,
And as for his arpeggios
What he's doing goodness knows!
I proposed that he might try the flute
He said he didn't 'give a hoot'.
He thought he'd rather try the harp,
I'm afraid my reply was rather sharp.
Perhaps my attitude's not right
And the cello might show him in a better light.
As you very well know
It's a little less than a month ago
Since he aimed a catapult at my cat
And I really can't put up with that!
I suggest you find him another tutor
I hope he doesn't go and shoot her!

Irene Igbinedion

DISPENSING THE PAST

I grew up within an unruling family
Being young and naive
All I knew was how to please
Years had been wasted
By trying to find myself
I married twice
Because I rolled that dice
A child was born into each one
But I ended each relationship
They were just a crack of a whip
My heart did slowly slip
So now I'd hit rock bottom
I threw away all that was rotten
Alone . . . I'd started anew
My friends were just a few
Rebuilding my bricks
They came with their sticks
And try to shatter my name
My existence they tried to frame
Again I had to carve and remould
Awful years I had to unfold
So now I'm facing those forces
And avoiding divorces
'Tis a waste of youth
Now I've learnt the truth
All was my doing
But I am not shooing
The very essence of me.

Suzan Gumush

THE DEBATE

What is happening? A debate,
She sits alone, pen in hand - debating with emotion . . .
She knows when she is positive and she doesn't think . . .
She is happy, but reality is emotional values . . .
She can sit listening to the outside world,
The sounds of the wind howling outside her window,
The veranda door rattling,
The sound of the ticking clock - the whistling in her ears,
The emotion in her heart - but she realises about the debate . . .
She takes a sip of tea,
She looks around again - she is in her home,
She sees a book on the floor - the one she has started to read,
At last she thinks - she has wanted to read it for a long time,
But she has been held up - by - the debate.
She sits and wonders if others are debating,
'Of course they are' she says,
Emotional values are with everyone,
What is happening? She is leaving them behind,
Moving on . . . but she thinks . . .
The others better leave me alone . . .

Josie Lawson

THE WIZENED TREE AND THE WIND

I lay beside the wizened tree
Its torrid limbs leaned over me
Brown be gnarled and gnarled the grey
Bark and leaves had turned to grey
And the wind blew gently

I stared up to the wizened bough
As bark unfurled as furrowed brow
Leaves were black and black was dead
They floated down around my head
And the wind sighed sadly

I gazed astern to wizened root
Entangled mass, corrupted moot
Corrugated limbs and limbs of hope
And the wind despaired sharply

I huddled to the wizened trunk
As shelf to bed and bed as bunk
Knots were eyes and eyes were dark
Into my soul they bored their mark
And the wind protested loudly

How long I lay beneath that tree
The wizened tree had wizened me
It cast its spell as naive I lay
It took my form and then walked away
I was the tree
I stand there still for the world to see
And laughed wizenly.

Carol Fisher

MORTAL LINKS

A generation's outing, a brilliant day in March
Granny, elder daughter, daughter's daughter Lily Darch
They walk the quay at Hartland, spy a fulmar's nest
(Lily is just three years old and talks her very best)

They picnic in a field upon the family rug
And spread out all the goodies from the ancient family trug
Later they hike to Stoke, view the churchyard stones
And read historic glimpses of long-disjointed bones

Mother's fingers trace the letters, wind-smoothed and lichen-green
Dispel the granite's fetters to read who may have been
Head, food and body stones with heavy load beneath
Of fatal births and fevers and shipwreck-stricken grief

Her voice is low, respectful with eternal fascination
Which attends the ends of others' lives, their final destination
She and Granny quietly muse upon the graveyard scene
Forget just for a moment their charge, the Lily queen

They hear a plainsong voice, see her touch a stone
And make out she is reading as her mother's done
'I'm sorry you are dead and cannot see your friends
But when you're bad you all get killed and that is how it ends!'

Amazed they gazed at Lily
Stunned to silence, well almost
'Holy Mother' Granny said
Lily's mother, 'Holy Ghost!'

V Jean Tyler

THE NINETEENTH HOLE

No doubt about it, the land was dry
yet the mountains were blue with heather:
the trees grew tall, the grass grew high,
the sun was hot - and even the weather
looked good, as billowing clouds of rain
amassed from the west, then passed again,
and the land lay, parched and dry.

So I dug me a hole to find a spring
to water the cattle and grow the corn.
Deep it was dug where the signs had led
but the drought remained, and the beasts lay dead.

Eighteen desperate holes we dug
growing weaker ourselves - how we needed rain.
Yet the trees grew tall, the grass grew high,
the birds sang on, and still the sky
gave promise of storms, but all in vain.

There *must* be water beneath the ground
to sustain the life that was all around.
'Move out. Move on,' the faint hearts said,
'Move quickly out or we'll all be dead.'

I stared at the mountains and said me a prayer
to the One who made them. 'Tell me where
they get their nourishment, for there *must*
be water about, or the land would be dust.'
Then I saw a fold where the grass grew green
under a rock which we had not seen.
'Dig there,' I said, striking in the pole,
and water gushed from the nineteenth hole.

Diana Morcom

RAS

You slept on my bed, sighed with contentment,
yawned, stretched out your body and smiled.
You crept up close to me, laid still, sleeping
close in the warmth of my arms.

You walked by my side, filled with enjoyment,
paused, pulled me along as you ran.
You ran over meadows, fields, stone pathways
close by the river or coolness and calm.

You frowned as you listened, gazed with discernment,
put your sweet puzzled head on one side.
You came sadly up to me, gently touching me
healing my wounds with your charms.

You went away from me, called my name in abandonment,
lost, your spirit came home to me here.
I came straight to the place I knew you would be,
called your name and you ran to my arms.

You looked up and kissed me, sighed with contentment,
put your paw on my shoulder and smiled.
You crept up close to me, laid shaking and trembling
safe my dear dog in the warmth of my arms.

Mary Farrant

SHADE TOO INDULGENT

Red balloon to flee Tim allowed.
He did not know why
and he gave a cry
when it leapt, ignoring the crowd.
It assumed a life of its own;
Tim sorrowfully wept;
quite sad and inept
he emitted petulant groan.
Tim's father, who wasn't too bad,
though he softly cursed,
blew up till he burst
one white - 'I want red!' yelled the lad.
It was, without doubt, a disgrace
to spoil his son so
but Dad had a go
at retrieve by floating in space.
Then lobster came somewhat later
all puffy and red
in sky overhead,
not what it seemed - it was Pater!
Threaded thro teeth floated a green
balloon, not a red;
'Don't grumble,' Mum said.
'Oh, Timothy, don't make a scene!'
Brave Dad, though distended, had flown;
whole clan colour blind,
why should Timmy mind;
this last was pale pink, had he known.

Ruth Daviat

His Day Out

When I said to my husband, 'Let's have a day out.'
I thought he might throw a tantrum and began to shout,
but all innocence he replied, 'I know just where to go.'
So we drove till we reached the Antique Car Show.

Hundreds of old cars had been brought for the rally,
all cleaned up and polished for the judging finale.
Their hand-painted bodywork gleamed in the sun.
Jim told me the name, age and make of each one.

A special edition Bentley attracted attention
and the Rolls Royce Cloud there was worth a mention.
Elfs, Minors and Stags were all lined up in sections,
the newer editions to the antique collections.

Young and old men were all in their glory
telling each other story upon story
of the good-old-days, when cars were cars,
with leather upholstery, wooden trims and chrome bars.

At the rally were old cars which I'd never seen,
my husband agreed it was the best one there'd been.
It mightn't have been how I'd planned the day,
but soon I was glad I'd decided to stay.

Petula Campbell

RAINDROPS

When raindrops fall from out the sky
Do you wonder where or why?
They may go or finish up
Maybe it is in your cup.
But on this day the raindrop fell
It fell right down into the well
Of cabbage leaves so green and lush.
It was quiet and no rush
Until the day the gardener came
Things would never be the same.
The raindrop cringed within the leaves
What was its fate? Then came the heaves
As the knife went through the heart
It tore the cabbage leaves apart.
Then from its safety of the well
Into a deep dark sink it fell
Down the plug hole, down the drain
Down the river that followed the lane
Until it was drawn by the sun
Into the sky to become one
Of the raindrops that would fall
Maybe this time it would hit a wall!

C V Chant

CAN TED COME TOO?

A few fond memories of my own childhood.
Alone and frightened there me stood.
I couldn't run and dared not to cry.
Withdrawn, but believed to be shy.
Beaten and bullied I learned to be tough.
People thought I'd gone from shy to rough,
But little did these people know.
Beaten so much in the dark I glowed.
Then the day finally arrived.
This is where I thrived.
A lady knocked on the door.
I knew I'd seen her somewhere before.
She wanted to have a little chat.
She wanted the truth. She wanted the facts.
Then a policeman took me away.
I was kind of sad that day.
Where I was going I never knew,
But remember asking if Ted could come too.
Abused as a child I thought I was bad.
I never returned, for this I'm glad.
Now I've children of my own,
And I've watched them carefully as they've grown.
I love them dearly more each day.
How proud and happy I could never say.

Sally A Swain

Cosmic Litterbugs

I watched this documentary on the tele
all about what's going on in space.
It explained about the manmade garbage
that orbits at an unbelievable pace.

They reckon since they started that's
going back nigh 40 year.
They've left 5000 tonnes of rubbish
up there where there's no air.

Well I phoned that lot at NASA
I said 'Tell me what's your game
don't you ever clear up behind you?
You should hang your heads in shame.'

They were really nice about it, said
'We want no international discord
next time we send the shuttle up
we'll put a couple of skips on board.
Have a nice day.'

John L Walker

A TERRIBLE TALE

Cotoneaster Blenderbland's
A child who's getting out of hand.
And though I spell it out in verse,
She's really gone from bad to worse.

She spat and kicked in history
And threw her homework up a tree!
In maths her sums were all to pot . . .
Did teacher like it? Not a lot!

When told to write a funny story
She hid in the lavatory,
Then set fire to all her books;
No wonder she got funny looks!

Back home, when Mum said, 'Come, be quick!'
She hit her with a hockey stick,
And wouldn't wear her woolly jumper,
Even though brother said, 'I'll thump her!'

And then she went on holiday
To Mud-on-Sea, ten miles away,
And frightened all the hotel guests
By screaming during quiet rests.

She got quite bold: did not care tuppence!
But soon she got her due comeuppance!
A lollipop she wished to try . . .
But fate, it seems, was standing by.

There were no lollies left in town,
She found, when wandering up and down.
The ice-cream man said, 'Never fret,
We've still got lots of cornets, yet.'

This last remark, it rose her hackles,
And thinking of past rugby tackles,
She stormed up to his van and said:
'I don't want ice-cream! Boil your head!'

She shouted at the ice-cream man
And carved her name upon his van.
Annoyed, he pushed (having no fear)
Cotoneaster off the pier!

David Blackburn

TROUBLE IN HEAVEN

God in heaven had his problems,
With rebelling angels in disgrace,
Satan, their leader, an evil emblem,
Was banished to a very hot place.

All is explained in the Bible,
When Satan desired to be Lord,
Hankering for knowledge and power,
And with many angels indulging in fraud.

God could have had them destroyed,
But relented and forgave their crimes.
All bad angels were expelled,
And ended up languishing in Hell.

All that was a long time ago,
Although traces of trouble still remain,
Natural disasters and disease still beset us,
And unpredictable calamities prevail.

Genetic interference with nature,
Spraying with poisonous things,
Where this will lead is conjecture,
That only the future can bring.

Milly Saunders

A Patient's Point Of View

'How are you today,' they ask, 'are you feeling better?
Do you want a cup of tea? Has someone sent a letter?
Shall we go out today, we could sit in the grounds'
But really it is not as nice in here as you think it sounds.

I cannot have my dog with me, or go out in my car
If allowed out for a walk I cannot go too far
They say that I am not myself, they say that I am ill
But I will get much better if I swallow one more pill.

I've never taken tablets, not for any sort of pain
But now I must rely on them or be told I'm insane.
Who has the right to tell me my mind is not quite right
And I must always be within the nurses' sight?

Why do I feel frustrated, why do I get so mad?
Why do I feel downhearted and sometimes very sad?
Is it because I know inside that there is nothing wrong?
I'm what's called hale and hearty and also very strong.

I wish that I could just go home where memories abound
To see my garden in full bloom and have my friends around
But is my house still waiting just in case some day
I'll be allowed to leave this place and go home to stay?

That is a hope I cling to through both day and night
A pleasant memory I still keep well within my sight
My life, I'm told, now depends on a Tribunal's point of view
So be very careful friend - one day it may be *you!*

Letitia Snow

A TASTE OF HEAVEN

I've been in the presence of angels,
where all was at peace,
all serene.
And my being was uplifted with calmness,
where once
chaos had reigned there supreme.

I have touched, and been touched
by my angels,
have both seen them and heard them as well,
I've been with them to places they visit
and saw the difference betwixt
Heaven and Hell.

They took me so softly, so gently,
to their Heaven
on that far distant shore,
there to meet friends and my loved ones,
who had journeyed there
a long time before.

I was welcomed with joyous enrapture,
and a great happiness
pervaded my soul
for I felt I could stay there forever
if ever I was asked
to enroll.

Such a privilege though
has to be worked for,
the Judgement upon which we're based.
I know now why my angels took me with them,
'twas to give me
that Heavenly taste.

John A Moore

FOREVER LOVE

The slim, auburn haired beauty,
met a tall, dark, handsome man,
could this be how it all began?

As they walked through streets
and fields they listened to
faraway bells that peeled.
Walking, talking, holding hands
these young lovers laid down
their plans.

They married in December so windy,
so cold this only proved their
love was bold.
They set up home in a few small
rooms, this was where their love bloomed.

The years rolled by and still in love,
watched over by the Lord above.
They provided their children with
their everlasting love.

Parted now but still together, with
fond memories and close hearts forever,
their love will never fade.
For the eternal flame of love still
lingers deep within her heart.

Michael James

UNDERSTAND THE BEGINNING

Beginning to feel despondent,
contemplating what next,
I stand and survey a spring morning.
Eastern sun flickers,
kindles a wilderness,
lights up lemon-green leaves
of one weeping willow planted twenty years ago,
a brittle stick of a dream, trusted to grow.
Memory fires imagination,
triggers an all-excluding task.

Beginning to feel elated,
understanding what next,
I plant and study fifty saplings.
Western sun filters flimsy stems,
liquid light trickles down,
dapples dark undergrowth.

With trust more trusting than a thirsty sapling,
truth more truthful than a living forest,
hidden thoughts, each one brighter than the last,
glow in the darkness, dim at first then radiant,
fan a quiver of green flames.

There will be mornings when I watch the sun
creep down to meet the silent stream,
soundless, only the tremolo of willows
will fill the spaces.
There will be evenings when I watch the moon
flood the forest with silver rivers,
endless, the silhouetted whispering of dreams.

Then, I will think of those who have
no willows and know that I am living.

Maureen Bold

ONLY A STRAY

I don't know when I haven't roamed the streets,
Been cold and hungry - never any treats,
Slinking from the people passing by
Through fear, there is no love for such as I.
Should any kind child give my head a pat
I'd hear remarks like 'Don't go too near that'
It's not my fault I have a mangy patch
And fleas don't go however much I scratch.

I'm soaking wet, most days don't feel too good,
A van's drawn up, I'll crawl beneath this wood,
A long stick's probing, 'Come on boy' I hear
And then there's something caught behind my ear,
'Can you reach him? Mind he doesn't bite'
They've yanked me out, I'm shaking now with fright,
Someone has picked me up, don't know what for,
I'm in the back and now they've closed the door.
It's stopped, must say I've quite enjoyed the ride,
Don't know what sort of building I'm inside,
My captor's left, I'm stroked and gently led
Inside a pen and now I'm being fed,
The lady's kind and worried that I'm thin,
I'll sleep if I can get used to the din!
I live here now, have never been so pleased,
The mange is better, gone are all the fleas,
I'm walked outside just for a little spell,
Not far because I'm still not very well.

My lady's brought me to the vet today,
I'll have to free his pain I hear him say,
She's cuddling me, no luckier dog than I,
I lick her tears and hear her say 'Goodbye.'

Pam Owers

ONCE UPON A HOLIDAY

A whirlwind bustle of packing.
'Don't forget your toothbrushes'
I yell at the kids.
'Is everyone ready?'
'Yeah Dad' they all reply.

The minibus is loaded,
and,
remembering to get the Gramps.
We're off!

Hoping the luggage is tied
down tight,
on the roof rack,
excited chattering in the back.

The packed lunches are unwrapped,
the tea spills over the map.
I blame the wife
she blames me,
the Gramps are having a nap.

Stopping to get petrol, in a service station
and joining the slowest queue,
looking at others, looking at us.
All fighting to get to the loo.

After several hours of frustration,
in traffic jams, and heat and dust,
we finally arrive at our destination.
We hurriedly unpack,
the kids hit the pool,
and we hit the sack.

Paul Kelly

DRAGONFLY

Poor dragonfly
Stuck on the ground
Unable to fly
On gold wings
Across the sky.
Poor dragonfly
I know that you're
About to die.
Why's it so hard
To help you die?
Such suffering.
There as you lie
Twitching, dying
Poor dragonfly
On the ground.
At last I choose
To help you die
A descending
Foot from the sky.
Once again off
Again you fly
A tiny spirit
Up in the sky.

Kaye Axon

THE BUSY BEES

Aunt Mathilda was as busy as a bee pressing her clothes
While so doing sang pretty ditties of life's pains and woes
Then in came Madam Queen Bee buzzing - a most unwelcome guest
'Shoo, shoo, you fool insect!' she screamed. 'You are such a
nasty pest!'

Aunt Mathilda tried to ignore the bee's buzzing as best as she could,
'Please go away you tearaway!' How she wished it would,
It darted onto the curtain, stumbled and fell.
'Oh, my dear Lord! Where is it now?' she yelled.

'I don't need this, I won't be stung for I have so much work to do.
Please exit!' She opened the window widely and made pleas anew.
It landed on her right arm and she shook it and yelled again at the
top of her voice,
Cousin Aubrey awakened by the din downstairs came to see why
there was this great noise.

'Get the insect repellent quickly, don't just stand there and stare!
Get off me you infidel, how dare you come so near!'
Cousin Aubrey grabbed it with a gloved hand and released it outside
Now everything is forgotten and in the locked room Aunt Mathilda
continues pressing clothes, admiring her completed works
with great pride.

Margaret Andrews

HEART ON THE SLEEVE

Love is the thing
To be put on display
Wear love so proudly
Do not lock love away
How would folk know
How would they believe
If love was not worn
Like a heart on the sleeve?
Love is not a thing
To be locked in a drawer
With all one's mementoes
Souvenirs kept galore
Love should be worn
Like a smile on your face
Not hidden away
In some dark dreary place
Love makes you feel wanted
Makes you feel blithe and gay
For when love is returned
Love just grows every day
Love is a passion you feel in the heart
Thrills and excitement and joy from the start
If you can help love to grow stronger each day
Love will stay with you forever, it will not go away
To your family, friends and sweetheart, husband or wife
If your nurture love daily
You will have love for life.

Eleanor Brandes-Dunn

LEWIS CARROLL

Lewis Carroll (1830 - 98) born Charles Lutwidge Dodgson
A lecturer in mathematics and Oxford don
The child of a country parson
Born in Daresbury in Cheshire - became an icon
Attended grammar school in Yorkshire and Rugby
Had a bad stammer and was very shy
Produced a home-made magazine of his own comic verse
Obtained a University post but found it difficult to converse
Preached only occasionally (1861) after his ordination
Produced maths text books and comic writing on an occasion

His first masterpiece 'Alice's Adventures Underground'
Later as 'Alice's Adventures in Wonderland' (1865) found
A book which children's literature did revolutionise
Putting all previous literary pieties aside - later did originate
'What Alice Did There' (1871) and 'Through The Looking Glass'
Along with another book of his class
'The Hunting Of The Shark'
After those his genius turned dark
His fame remained to grow
Best works recurring to show

Ann Copland

LOVE'S LABOURS LOST (AGAIN)

Star crossed we were,
like Shakespeare's soon widowed pair.
Families defied
for meetings quick snatched and rare.
No balcony, of course, just a quiet cafe
witnessed our love grow deep and seek to find a way
to share life's precious hours.

A flower, a gift
sealed our close affinity
as, like those two,
we embraced eternity.
Oh, brief and radiant time when, blissfully unaware
of whispered plotting that makes love's friend cry 'beware',
romance built dreamy towers.

Then, swift despair
at a sudden, cruel curfew.
To meet no more,
deny ever knowing you.
It could not, must not be, our hasty notes declared.
A midnight tryst would prove each to each that we dared
challenge unfeeling powers.

They killed that dream,
saying it was 'for our good'.
Our age cried halt.
Cold sense won, if naught else could.
Now, entombed among the undead eighty pluses,
we have only memories of when racing pulses
made our story as theirs
- but an aged Romeo and Juliet.

Celia Andrews

PASTICHE FROM A BAR STOOL PERCH

He walked in alone,
   Found a space at the crowded bar
And ordered up his drink.
   Not very tall, well dressed,
A nice tan, good head of hair,
   Platinum, as some men go.
Not much over fifty I would say;
   But the eyes were blank
And the body language spoke
   Of a man deserted.
The strained face and parted lips
   Betrayed an inner hurt.
Trying his best to look
   As if he belonged there.
Looking mostly straight ahead
   As if to find some interest
In the row of bottles
   Upturned on their measly optics.
Or perhaps not seeing them at all
   But behind the blank eyes
Reliving bits of other days.
   And no one spoke to him
As he carefully drank his beer,
   Put down the glass
And moved off out to somewhere else.
   Another passing ship,
Another night.

G Baker

EVERYTHING STOPS FOR TEA?

During the darkest days of war
People would rush to the shelter door,
Beneath the street they'd hurry down
When bombs were falling on London town.
There they would stay all through the night
Hoping and praying with all their might
That they would live to see tomorrow
And think of nice warm beds with sorrow.
They'd sing some songs to cheer themselves up
But more important they'd have a cup
Of that fine brew, dark and sweet,
That the British drink when troubles they meet.
In vacuum flasks they brought it down
When bombs were falling on London town.
One night, so my old gran did tell,
There came to that dark underground cell
A mother and daughter loud and brash.
But the girl turned out to be rather rash,
For when the bombs fell thick and fast
She found their tea was not to last.
'Ooh Ma,' she wailed, 'we've run out of tea
Back home to make some I'll quickly flee.'
Her mother paled and screeched 'Oh Lil
You've made me feel so very ill.
If you go out there you'll die for sure,
For the sake of tea you'll be no more.
Now while I see you've got some grit,
Oh 'tain't werf it Lil, 'tain't werf it.'
Poor Lil sat down and looked forlorn,
For her tea she'd have to wait till dawn.

Patricia Smith

DEREHAM DOWN

In the valley of Dereham Down
once a busy cotton town
now the mills no longer hum
to feed the worker from the slum
prosperity has fled

The cobbled streets are sprouting grass
that echoed clogs to morning mass
no laughter at the local inn
no tankard frothing at the brim
a ghost-town of the dead

Deserted streets and alleyways
so hard to picture market days
all so quiet, all so still
even the wind has time to kill
and rustles leaves of red

Factory chimneys rearing high
like grimy fingers to the sky
and pointing state accusingly
why have my people gone from me
and give me up for dead

R G Stevens

BLUE

Here I am feeling rather blue
I ask myself, do I still love you?
We do have good times, we also have bad
but do the happy times outweigh the sad.
I know you love me, I know you care
my heart is not a merry-go-round, like on a fair.
Pulling on my heartstrings, this is not a game
you can only pull for so long, then there's pain.
My life revolves around you in every which way
you say you want to leave, then you want to stay.
This feeling blue is making me see red
you're twisting my mind and it's hurting my head.
Mind games are cruel and making us both mad
why do we do this it's making us both sad.
I'm constantly thinking and torturing my mind
do you still love me or are you being kind?
Some big questions need to be asked
which will be a long and arduous task.
I do need you to be there when I feel blue
I cannot do this alone especially without you.
So let's get together and talk about this
let's make up with a cuddle and a loving kiss.

J E Royle

THE PROSPEROUS SOUL

'Don't take me down that road again'
of hardship, hurt and haze,
I fell so many times upon its poverty displays
it reshaped my shell with pains of hell
and starved my inner soul
of practical ability to achieve its dreams and goals.
Halt! I refuse to take your strangling out-stretched hand again,
and push on with a surge of determination
pouring through my members
saturating me to the bone.
As I ignore the offer of your prison cell
I find myself in grounds much wider
where I can breathe
and have space to unfold my untried wings
how they have ached to stretch to life.
My soul does prosper in these 'fields of potential'
where it can stretch its legs
from the crush of the world's womb
that did hold it 'in its place',
for now I am born again into 'myself'
and now know, as any new-born,
all my choices lay afresh before me.
As before I did say 'Don't take me down that road again'
now I say 'I will not let you take me down that road again'
and no 'force' shall persuade my decision,
for I will, will 'it' to be buried at sea.
Now I can dance in my dress of Sunday best
for I have legs, like I never had legs before,
and swim in waters that hold the good things of life.
Now, with stretching wings, with eagles I soar.

R M H

THE WAY THINGS ARE IS NOT THE WAY

The way things are is not the way:
It's with regret I have done wrong.
What's meant to be will be one day.

My mind is trapped in disarray,
Who mislaid the words to my song?
The way things are is not the way.

In the hands of fate I am clay;
Prize fools I've found myself among.
What's meant to be will be one day.

Take me home I don't want to stay,
I'm claustrophobic in this throng.
The way things are is not the way.

Multiplying crowd starts to sway;
Sweat down my back I don't belong.
What's meant to be will be one day.

If there's a God to Him I say:
Purge my weakness and make me strong.
The way things are is not the way,
What's meant to be will be one day.

Pauline Ilsley

MURMURED HEARTBEATS

Lost but never forgotten
Afraid but yet so unsure
Endangered as your life fades away before you
Unseen as your heart beats no more.

A small grass verge you walked upon
Before your life faded away with the sun
As your head became heavy and body so weak
A last thought in your mind was of your family.

You can hear the hounds of hell barking
As you crawl to save your cubs
'Who will feed my family?'
Please help 'I can't walk, I can't run.'

You can only fight for freedom
For all creatures great and small
You realise your wounds are weeping so deep
As your world now lies in your soul.

E Snell

THE MAN AT THE CHURCHYARD GATE

I was late. Quickly I made for the old church on the hill,
with its towering steeple, ancient stained glass glinting light.
'Right,' I thought, 'I'm late. The doors will be closed, the stewards
seated, then I'll walk in, rousing people from prayer. What a pity,
I should have been there.'

Sunset's glow outlined houses on the hillside with gold as I felt
the first chill of autumn in the air. I was cold.
thus preoccupied - and late - I glanced up, at the churchyard gate, and
saw, lit by the sunlight's glare, a bearded figure, standing there.

Tall in stature, staff in hand, gazing out across the land,
sad eyes weeping, long brown hair, in the sunset, standing there.
When I reached the church at last, as the graves I hurried past,
glancing back I hoped that He, might stand near the poplar tree.
But no sign of Him I saw, as I walked towards the door, then a sign
in evening light; 'Service cancelled, for tonight'.

Richard Langford

OUR KITTEN

He was white and black, his name was Shmoo
Very special was he, of 'the' select few.
Who managed to live, not be put in a bucket,
My son was visiting, and home he took it.
Too young was he, to leave his mum
Protected, his love, he gave to my son.
Within the week he was drinking and eating,
Appointment was made, for his first meeting,
With the vet of course, to check him over
A little ball of fluff, we took and showed her.
His antics, always made us laugh,
As he gambolled and fell up the garden path.
He had no fear, we always kept an eye
I think that cat 'thought' he could fly,
Always 'jumping and leaping' on this and that,
That was Shmoo, our kitten, our well loved cat.
As he got older, he grew tall and long
Never missed once, the dinnertime gong,
Until the day came, when he never returned
We called, we all worried, our stomachs all churned.
We looked for weeks, our neighbours helped too,
Will 'never' forget our cat called Shmoo.
He was just six months when he left us, hadn't grown up really at all,
Such a good puss, who liked loads of fuss, 'You're missed', still
                                        listen for your call.

Beverley Diana Burcham

'ARMAGEDDON'

I awoke to the sound of battle.
I had been wounded in the neck,
and all around me
lay the dead and the injured.

Those who survived, fought on,
and screamed abuse at the enemy.
Some threw stones and hid in caves,
others huddled together in the dark shadows,
and convinced themselves of victory.

Their captain grew impatient.
He stood surrounded by generals and lieutenants,
who stood in line, disguised in black hoods and cloaks,
their yellow eyes flashing in the thick, misty,
congealing air.

He yelled, 'Forward!'
to his battle-weary troops,
but somehow, despite his mask of arrogance,
there seemed to exist an undercurrent
of inevitable defeatism.

'Forward!'

He knew his doom.
He read the book.

Ken Price

THE NIGHT OF THE BALL

Gay laughter and soft music filled the air on the night of the ball
As the Lady Anne danced with her lover, her lover so handsome
and tall.
Then suddenly the dancing stopped as the door flung open wide
and a hooded figure entered in, a pistol by his side,
'I claim the Lady Anne,' he said. 'No other shall she wed.'
and raising his pistol in the air he shot her lover dead.
Out of the hall the Lady Anne ran and into the woods to hide.
Her one intent to escape from this man, the man who would make her
his bride.
The tall trees hid the stars from view, no light to show the way,
Only the sound of the distant waves as they lapped in the sheltering bay.
The shrubs tore at her silken dress and sharp stones cut her feet,
As she stumbled blindly through the woods in a panic of retreat.
The sound of a riding horseman, fast gaining as she ran,
Struck terror deep and lent speed to the feet of the lovely Lady Anne.
For he had killed her lover, no mercy had he shown
And now he rode in hot pursuit to claim her for his own.
The tall trees shook their leafy heads and bent their branches low,
As if to tell the Lady Anne she should no further go.
The wind blew hard into her face as if it tried to say,
'Go back, go back, it is not safe for you to go this way.'
But on she ran unheeding, filled with terror, grief and fright,
Straight into the arms of her lover on that cold and starry night.
They found her next day at the foot of the cliff, her body washed up
by the tide
And folk tell to this day of the tragic way, and the night that the
Lady Anne died.
The old house is now standing empty, well empty, not quite, folk recall.
Though no one has lived in that large empty house since that night, the
night of the ball.

But if you pass by when the moon's at its height
As it was long ago on that tragic night,
In the arms of her love, still so handsome and tall,
The two figures glide through the now empty hall.
To the music that played on the night of the ball.

Evelyn Tilley

THE JOY GALORE

This was to be my maiden voyage on board the *'Joy Galore'*,
I never crewed nor laid my shoe,
Upon a boat before.
With teary eye, I waved goodbye to Jane upon the shore.

I sucked a sweet, as I'd been told seasickness spoils a day,
And so I chewed, my eyes were glued,
Fast on the rising waves.
Jack slapped my back with such a whack and cried, 'We're
on our way!'

The salty sea washed on the decks, the wind rushed in the sails,
And *'Joy Galore'*, she seemed to soar
Amid a northerly gale,
A flying ship, that soared and dipped, above the sand and shale.

At times it felt my heart would rise and hasten to my throat,
My hands would shake, with every break,
Of wave upon the boat,
But Jack was kind, he said, 'Unwind!' and furnished me with hope.

'The *'Joy Galore'* can ride the waves while you and me shall steer,
We'll helm in turns and thus discern
The joys, the hopes and fears.'
His words were balm, they made me calm, we broke into the beers.

How fast did I promote myself to salt-baked mariner?
With weary bones I staggered home,
A spectral tide roared in my ears,
I rocked and swayed as still on waves, Jane blamed it on the beer.

Gemma Gill

A Baby's Born...

A baby's born, he cries his first,
Then mother's milk he will thirst.
Six months later, he can shout,
One year later he's about.

Five years on, he'll start school
When Mother leaves, then he'll drool.
At ten years old he hears his call,
Nothing matters but football.

Five years later he's got some spots,
Nothing bad, they're just little dots.
At twenty years, he's a big strong man,
He's on his own, Mum's done all she can.

At twenty-five he's got a wife of his own,
With a new baby son in their comfortable home.
A baby's born, he cries his first,
Then mother's milk he will thirst.

Andrew Williamson

TITANIC

A spectacular event as Titanic left that quay,
Bound for America, a port she'd never see,
She was invincible, unsinkable they said,
No one ever guessed, that tragedy lay ahead.

Temperatures dropped as the sun sank low,
Wining, dining, merriment carried on below,
Families in their cabins settle for the night,
April 4th, 1912, last time Titanic saw daylight.

In the moonless sky, the chill winds bite,
A mountain of ice, was moving into sight,
'Iceberg ahead!' lookouts cry to the crew,
Sounding he bell, loud the whistle blew.

Quartermaster Murdock received the report,
Fast, reversed the engines, steered her to port,
The vital message came seconds too late,
Ship struck the iceberg signing her fate.

A clash of ice and steel, as plating starts to tear,
Oceans of freezing water flooding everywhere,
Lifeboats quickly lowered, Captain cabled SOS,
Firing up the rockets, Titanic's in distress.

Listing to port, tilted down toward the bow,
Cries from steerage decks, there's people trapped below,
Smokestacks shutting down, engines slowly die,
Titanic rose 200 feet into the starlit sky.

A massive roar of thunder, Titanic broke in two,
Amid screams of terror, she slipped away from view,
Unnatural calm settled, over the cruel black sea,
Atlantic Ocean bed, was now, Titanic's destiny.

M L Broadbent

MY SISTER'S DRESS - THE LAST WORD

I said it was blue
She said it was green
That dress full of spots
In its clear polythene

This dispute went on
All through Saturday
As it hung on a hanger
Up on display.

The time became due
To go out for the evening
I said it was blue
Just as she was leaving

She hissed, 'It's green.'
As she closed the door
My chance was gone
To say anything more.

But I had to have
The very last word
And though this may sound
Quite absurd,

I put on her pillow
A little note
Just the word 'blue '
On it, I wrote.

B Jane Laycock

GONE FISHING

When fishing tales we start to tell
There is just one, I remember well
When remembered I think with pride.
Of that sunny day, I, caught a fish alive

Stood by the man with an experienced eye
Who threw out the bait and tied the fly
We cast our lines to the silver stream
Sun dancing on ripples as in a dream

Watching the water shimmer and flicker
A tug on the line, and a heart beat quicker
The bobbing float was no longer there
Cries of excitement filled the air

A pull at the line, two hands came to hold
Sure I'd caught a monster big and bold
Out came the keepnet, sleek and green
To imprison, the smallest tiddler, ever seen

Though sad is the day and heavy the heart
As we say goodbye, the stories start
Of the quiet man who stood by our side
On that hot summer's day, I caught a fish alive

And if there is Heaven for us to see
We are sure to know just where he'll be
In a shady nook by the silver stream
Quite contentedly, catching the rising bream.

Elizabeth Skidmore

THE MOUNTAIN

They walked around the mountain, its low slopes hanging green,
And gazed upon the pinnacle; its tip was never seen.
They gazed upon the mountain, and their anguish grew apace,
As they knew within that instant they must span its white-clad face.

The village was agin them, but could not make them stay,
And they made the first slopes early on the morning of that day;
The village stopped to watch them as they crawled across the ice,
Yet when the leader floundered they could not hear his voice.

And in that eerie silence the watchers held their breath;
To see this gallant party as it hurtled to its death.
Then someone broke the silence; a woman wailed aloud:
The men they all raced forward from the shocked and frightened crowd.

They climbed that mountain sadly, to where the last steps led,
And placed the broken bodies upon the well-worn sled.
The mountain took them gladly; the mountain took them all;
And not one sole survivor from that tragic snow-blind fall.

Corrie Francis

JANE AND THE FOX

'Jane dear, you know I never had to say
Tidy your room! It always stayed that way.
But now that you've a car, my dear, your boot!
You simply treat it like a rubbish chute!'
'Well Mum, it's Punch!' Her pony's name was Punch
And every day, she took him hay for lunch,
His pail, his head stall, saddle, bridle, coats;
A broken trough behind a sack of oats
Made Mother hoot! 'The kitchen sink! My dear,
It's not the multi-storey I should fear!
From Tesco to your car's a far worse route -
I never know what might jump out your boot!'

Jane found Punch tearing up the paddock's length -
To catch and calm him down took all her strength!
And then she understood - the hunt was out,
She heard the hooves, the tumult, all the shout;
Behind the hedge, the slavering masses flew
Hot on the fox's trail - and the hounds too.
She fumed, 'They might have let me know
To keep Punch in, 'stead of this rodeo!'
Went to the boot, and opened wide the lid -
Loosened some hay for Punch, and as she did
A red-brown streak flashed through the air, and in -
Frantic to get to earth, and save its skin!

Jane shut the lid - she didn't see!
(She might have done it anyway!)
At Tesco's, opened up the boot -
The fox shot out into a wood!
Her mother calmly watched it go -
'Well Jane, I always told you so!'

Marjorie R M Clark

Jordan's Grandmother's Story

When I was a girl I went to the fair,
And met the Young Farmers that were there;
Walked club lambs in, with tails still long;
I should have known that something was wrong.
The farmers thought it quite a yarn;
Six lambs had had the run of the farm.
They gave me a quizzical, sidelong glance;
I didn't know then I'd lost my chance.

Another year I went to the fair,
In stiletto heels on the grass there.
I searched the faces of farmers in rows,
And looked at the stalls selling dung coloured clothes.
My heart-throb came by, he nodded, and then
Walked over and looked into the sheep pen.
I went on home quite down in the mouth;
Wasting is this way a part of my youth.

The whole family went to the field of the fair,
My daughter, Jordan's mother, was there.
On bonfire night, like a lot of sheep,
We followed the crowd down South Street.
Old flames' faces were illumined in light,
While whistling of rockets disturbed the night;
When Jordan was a twinkle in his dad's eye,
And Catherine wheels lit up the sky.

When I went with Jordan to the fair,
They'd sold all but rams when we got there.
The entrance was then a muddy track,
With Scania lorries backing back.
We turned to go through, up Kingsway,
But trailer queues blocked the route that day.
The farmers were leaving, then I could see,
Their life had never been for me.

Maxine Bracher

SUBMISSIONS INVITED
SOMETHING FOR EVERYONE

POETRY NOW 2000 - Any subject,
any style, any time.

WOMENSWORDS 2000 - Strictly women,
have your say the female way!

STRONGWORDS 2000 - Warning!
Age restriction, must be between 16-24,
opinionated and have strong views.
(Not for the faint-hearted)

All poems no longer than 30 lines.
Always welcome! No fee!
Cash Prizes to be won!

Mark your envelope (eg *Poetry Now*) *2000*
Send to:
Forward Press Ltd
Remus House, Coltsfoot Drive,
Woodston,
Peterborough, PE2 9JX

OVER £10,000 POETRY PRIZES
TO BE WON!

Judging will take place in October 2000